The Whore Of Babylon

Judy C. Newton

Montgomery Publishing House

Montgomery Publishing House

America will ride the back of the Beast system and control it through the United Nations until about the middle of the Tribulation period. She will along with the rest of the world enforce the Mark of the Beast and the killing of Jews and Christians until the blood of the Christians runs so deep within her that God has had enough, then he will put into the hearts of the 10 Kings who support the Anti-christ to rise up and bomb her and completely destroy New York City in one hour along with disabling the rest of America. Then the Anti-christ will rise up and rule the world for the last 3 ½ years with nobody else to control or stop him.

CONTENTS

Babylon The Great, the mother of harlots and abominations of the Earth. (Rev. 17:5)

1

AMERICA THE BEAUTIFUL

God bless America land that I love. Stand beside her, and guide her thru the night with a light from above. From the mountains, to the prairies, to the oceans, white with foam; God bless America, my home sweet home.

And God did bless America. She rose from nothing to the greatest nation upon the earth in only 200 years. She sits as a queen upon the waters of the world in military might, influence, world dominance, and in global trade and commerce. All nations envy her, and all nations stand in awe of her.

She has the largest deep sea port in the world where nations come from all over to trade. Merchants sell goods and gain their wealth from her. She is the mightiest End-Time nation in the world.

She is dressed in fine linen, purple and scarlet, and glittering with gold, precious stones and pearls! Within her are the most prosperous people in the world. She throws table scraps away that the rest of the world would give anything to have for a meal.

Within her stands New York City where she rules the nations of the world through the United Nations Headquarters.

She indeed control's the world and governs its affairs. God has made her the head and not the tail. He has put her on top and not on the bottom. No military might dares to come against her.

God has indeed blessed America and that is his way. He said that if a nation would serve him and honor his ways that he would bless that nation. America was founded upon God's laws. Men and women came to the New World from England so they could be free to serve God the way they chose to without restrictions.

Our founding fathers created the Bill of Rights for every American and the Constitution of the United States to be the guide for us to live by. They founded this land stating, "Upon God we trust". They founded it as a constitutional republic not a democracy or a dictatorship. It was created for the people, by the people not for the government, by the government.

They placed laws in force that protected the American people against the tyrannical dictatorship of the government that they had been under in England.

Many times the world has grown cold toward the things of God and by God's mercy and grace he would send prophets, teachers, and leaders that would rise up and lead the people into a great outpouring of God's Spirit that would revive the people and cause them to turn back to God.

God sent:

Justin Martyr (A.D. 100-165)

Irenaeus (A.D. 125-200)

The Montanists (156-157 A.D)

Stewarton and Kirk of Shotts (1625-1630)

Moravians (1727)

Jonathan Edwards (1734)

George Whitefield (1727-1747)

Great Awakening – (1792)

The Amherst College Revival (1823)

Great Awakening – (1830)

Great Awakening – (1857)

Great Awakening – (1880)

Revival at Skye (1882)

Azusa Street Revival-(1905)

Welsh Revival – (1906)

Hebrides (1968)

The Argentinian Revival (1954, 1982)

The Asbury Revival (1970)

The Brownsville Revival (1995)

Some of God's instruments of Revival were:

John Alexander Dowie (1847-1907)

Dwight L. Moody (1850)

Charles Fox Parham (1873-1929)

Frank Bartleman   (1871-1936)

William Seymour (April 18, 1906)

William H. Durham (1873-1912)

Maria Woodworth-Etter (1844-1924

John G. Lake (1907))

Aimee Semple McPherson (1890-1944)

William Branham (1946)

Oral Roberts (1947)

Leonard Ravenhill (1950)

Kathryn Kuhlman (1954)

A.A. Allen (1955)

David Wilkerson (1952)

Steve Hill (1995)

God sent many others to stir up the people to return to God, and the people were sensitive to the Spirit of God and did turn back to God so God was able to continue blessing America.

But, then something terrible happened to America. She began to harden her heart against the things of God. She began to grow full of pride and began to lean upon her own arm and strength. She began to do things her way and to make her own laws and rules that did not submit unto God's. She began to throw off God's rule and anything that had to do with his laws.

The devilish teaching of Evolution began seeping into the school system as early as the late 19th century. Prior to that creation was taught in nearly all schools in the United States, often from the position that the literal interpretation of the Bible is inerrant. With the widespread acceptance of the theory of evolution in the

1860s after being first introduced in 1859, and developments in other fields such as geology and astronomy, public schools began to teach science that was reconciled with Christianity by most people, but considered by a number of early fundamentalists to be directly at odds with the Bible.

The deception that God might not have really created the universe was accepted in America and taught to our children in the school systems.

On June 25, 1962, the United States Supreme Court decided in Engel v. Vitale that a prayer approved by the New York Board of Regents for use in schools violated the First Amendment by constituting an establishment of religion. The following year, in Abington School District v. Schempp, the Court disallowed Bible readings in public schools for similar reasons. These two landmark Supreme Court decisions centered on the place of religion in public education, and particularly the place of Protestantism, which had long been accepted as the given American faith tradition.

America no longer wanted God to be taught as the creator of the universe and they did not want him to be prayed to in our school systems.

The New York school children who prompted the Engel vs. Vitale ruling had simply prayed: "Almighty God, we acknowledge our dependence on thee and beg thy blessing over us, our parents, our teachers and our nation."

America has experienced radical decline in each of the four areas which the children's prayer touched upon: youth, family, education, and national life. Minor recovery has occurred only since 1980 when the election of President Reagan brought forth a renewed emphasis on "traditional" values.

The removal of prayer from our schools was a violation of the third commandment which commands us "not to take the name of the Lord in vain." By the judicial act of forbidding invocation, the Court audaciously elevated a secularized system of education beyond the authority, reach and blessing of God himself. Worse than taking the Lord's sacred name in vain is treating it with contempt, denying it rightful place and stripping it from public use and even from the lips of children. Jesus' own expressed desire, "Let the little children come to me, and do not forbid them" was also violated by these judges, many of whom were raised in Christian homes.

But there was actually a gross violation of the third commandment by the U.S. Supreme Court a year earlier. A ruling in 1961, paved the way for stripping the Lord's name from our children's lips. In Torcaso vs. Watkins, the court overruled a provision of the Maryland Constitution which made "a declaration of belief in the existence of God" mandatory for holding public office.

Roy R. Torcaso, a Maryland resident and an avowed atheist, was refused a notary public commission when he would not subscribe to the required oath. His case was brought before the U.S. Supreme Court. The Court ruled to sanction atheism and overruled the Maryland Constitution.

These two events have created a generation of children and young adults that want nothing to do with the God of the Bible and have thrown him out of their lives.

Abortion was prohibited in 30 states and legal under certain circumstances (such as pregnancies resulting from rape, incest, and date drug.) in 20 states. The Supreme Court 1973 decision Roe v. Wade invalidated all of these laws, and set guidelines for the availability of abortion.

The definition of partial-birth abortion in H.R. 1833 is "an abortion in which the person performing the abortion partially vaginally delivers a living fetus before killing the fetus and completing the delivery." A number of physicians were involved in the drafting of this language to ensure that it is medically accurate and does not encompass any other form of abortion or legitimate medical procedure.

A registered nurse witnessed several partial-birth abortions while working for an abortionist. She described one of these abortions in a July 9, 1995, letter to Congressman Tony Hall: The baby's body was moving. His little fingers were clasping together. He was kicking his feet. All the while his little head was still stuck inside. Dr. Haskell took a pair of scissors and inserted them into the back of the baby's head. Then he opened the scissors up. Then he stuck the high-powered suction tube into the hole and sucked the baby's brains out.

This friend is what our President Obama is trying to make legal. It was banned in 2003 and Obama is trying to overturn this ruling. Obama deemed the PBA Ban "clearly unconstitutional" in a 2004 fundraising appeal signed by surrogate Michelle, "that must be overturned." In 1997, Obama voted against SB 230, which would have turned doctors into felons by banning so-called partial-birth abortion, & against a 2000 bill banning state funding. In 2004 Michelle Obama signed a campaign letter urging Illinois voters to elect her husband to the U.S. Senate in her letter, Michelle specifically mentioned the repeal of the Partial-Birth Abortion Ban Act as a desirable objective and as a cause to which Senator Barack Obama will be devoted: These partial birth abortions continue in our nation despite of the 2003 law banning them and Obama is trying to get it legalized.

Nothing hurts the heart of father God more than the harm to innocent children and this partial birth abortion is nothing more than murder of thousands of innocent children. We allow this in America and turn our heads and look the other way as this continues. America has blood on her hands that she will have to give account to God for.

The America that we have all known and loved is gone. She is gone forever!

I know this is hard to accept. We have always seen her bounce back to the things of God. But she will not bounce back this time. She has gone too far. She has rejected the God of the Bible for too long and has created her own gods.

Like the Children of Israel in the wilderness who created the golden calf, danced before it and cried to it to lead them, America has created her own gods of silver, gold, fame, fortune, greed, materialist, lust and power and she is bowing down before them, saying "lead us into pleasure and happiness". These be our gods oh America!

The television shows that we all loved to watch in the past that showed a Christian America such as, Leave it to Beaver, My Three Sons, The Walton's, Little house on the Prairie, Happy Days, and The Andy Griffith Show have been replaced with the Helen DeGeneres show, (approval of gays) The Oprah

Winfrey show, (New age movement) demons, devils, vampire and zombie shows.

The days are gone of leaving your keys in your car or your house unlocked. People kill each other now just for the fun of it.

Yes the heart of America has certainly changed. It has hardened itself against God and wants to be lovers of pleasures more than lovers of God. This has opened up the door for every devil and demon of hell to be unleashed upon her.

She will never be revived again to her full capacity of being a "Christian Nation". The Christians have been outnumbered! We are now the minority.

The America that we have all loved has fallen! She has fallen! America is no longer a Christian nation!

With the election of Barack Obama as president, the America we have loved and known for generation upon generation as a nation of individuals free from government control and ownership of our lives is gone.

Those of us who believe in the virtues that made this country great, self-reliance, hard work, entrepreneurship, individual liberty and responsibility are now strangers and a minority in our own country.

Christianity use to be the accepted religion of America and it is now looked down upon and called the right extremists and a terrorist's religion. America is trying to eradicate it altogether calling it a hate religion. This is because the heart of America has grown so cold and filled with evil spirits that they do not want anything or anyone around that will tell them what they are doing is wrong. They do not want Christianity around because it shines a light on the error of their ways and men's hearts are filled with darkness.

2

NO LONGER A CHRISTIAN NATION

America is no longer a Christian nation. Those who are true Christians have been outnumbered by the atheists, the homosexuals, the Muslims and every other Hodge Podge of faith. Protestant Christianity use to be the given religion of America. It is now the minority. The voice of the born again Christian is small and cannot be heard over the voice of the others and her vote is not great enough to ever make another lasting change in America.

In June 2006, President Obama made a speech in which he said, "Whatever we once were, we are no longer a Christian nation – at least, not just, we are also a Jewish nation, a Muslim nation, a Buddhist nation, and a Hindu nation, and a nation of nonbelievers." This statement was followed up in his inaugural address when he said, "For we know that our patchwork heritage is strength, not a weakness." Then, in April of this year, President Obama stated at a press conference in Turkey that Americans "do not consider ourselves a Christian nation, or a Muslim nation, but rather, a nation of citizens who are bound by a set of values." As Obama said in his speech: He did not want to acknowledge to Muslims worldwide that our country is very solidly established on Judeo-Christian principles, instead he said boldly, "Whatever we once were, we are no longer a Christian nation".

To think our forefathers fought and died for the right for our nation to be a Christian Nation–and to have this man say with pride that we are no longer that and to say that it is our strength! Obama telling the Muslims worldwide, "Whatever we once were, we are no longer a Christian nation" — is a bold attack on our Constitution.

So, what has happened to America? How can this really be happening to her? How can she change from a Christian nation to a nation that no longer wants God?

Sin has crept in little by little, and the government has taken away our personal liberties little by little until we have ended up in an America that is on its way to being ran by Hitler's and communists.

Because of gross sin in America God's timetable has begun to bring about the soon return of his son to earth and the 4 horses of the Apocalypse have been released. The first horse being the white horse was released upon the world in 2008 when Obama first became president of the United States. The second, third, and fourth horses have also been released. Worldwide wars, famines, and pestilence have been released upon the world. The wars will get worse and worse until we are in WWIII. Famine and hunger will get worse until only the Mark of the Beast is offered to be able to obtain food and medicine.

The white horse is the spirit of the Anti-christ that has gone forth into all of the world conquering and to conquer. It is the spirit of Islam that is taking over the world one country at a time. It will eventually be headed up by the Anti-christ himself who is alive and well on planet earth.

The Apostle Paul told us that in the last days we were to look for two things:

First: a great falling away of God's people from the faith.

Second: The appearance of the Anti-Christ.

Don't be fooled by what they say. For that day (The Rapture) will not come until there is a great rebellion against God and the man of lawlessness is revealed--the one who brings destruction. (2.Thess.2:3 NLT).

Paul says "Don't be fooled!" Jesus Christ will not come back to earth until there is a great falling away of God's people from the faith. This falling away would be so great that Paul likened it to the event of the Anti-Christ himself appearing.

We are in this rebellion right now. We are experiencing the greatest falling away from traditional family values and Christianity that we have ever seen. The very ones that use to stand up for the truths of the Bible are now saying that the gay lifestyle is acceptable by God. The Pope has just announced that the Roman Catholic Church is now going to accept the gay lifestyle, abortions, and divorcees. The Pope said their stance on these issues has been too strict in the past and they need to get their minds off of these issues and just accept everyone as they are.

The whole attitude of America and is being accepted by a lot of Christians is that we are now living in a new era and we should accept the gay lifestyle into our workplaces, homes, schools, and churches.

This has happened because false teaching has crept into the Church. Our leaders have been deceived by demons and devils and the pure word of God has been diluted with false doctrines.

Now the Holy Spirit tells us clearly that in the last times some will turn away from the true faith; they will follow deceptive spirits and teachings that come from demons. (1 Tim 4:1 NLT)

There is a new movement now called, "NALT". It is called the "Not All Christians Like That Project". This is a group that is forming at rapid speed they are Christians that believe in the gay lifestyle. They want the world to know that they are not the narrow minded Bible thumping Christians and that not all Christians are haters. They teach: If you are gay or lesbian, bisexual or transgender, then there's a good chance that you've either met a Christian or been confronted by the Christian-perspective that tells you "you are an abomination to God," or, "The Bible clearly is opposed to homosexuality," or something similar and there are Christians out there that are not like that! They are putting a brand new label on the word "Christian".

This know also, that in the last days perilous times shall come.

For men shall be lovers of their own selves, covetous, boasters, proud, blasphemers, disobedient to parents, unthankful, unholy, without natural affection (gay) trucebreakers, false accusers, incontinent, fierce, despisers of those that are good, (hatred for Christians) traitors, heady, high minded, lovers of pleasures more than lovers of God; Having a form of godliness, but denying the power thereof: from such turn away. (2 Tim. 3:1-5)

The doctrines of demons and devils have infiltrated the Church and she has become compromised and lukewarm. She has been seduced by the world. Her mind has been blinded and her heart has grown cold.

Obama has changed America forever and there is no going back. He has made laws that have continually broken our Constitution and no one is stopping him! I watch him use his "Executive Order" to break the Constitution and watch as no one, not even Congress can stop him. No one can stop him because he is empowered by a power that is not of this world. He is powered by Satan and Satan has given Obama his seat and his great authority. Obama is doing his own will not the will of God or the people and he is bringing Islam into America and taking away our personal rights one blow at a time.

Jesus himself spoke of Obama coming to the world just like Satan falling from the heavens in Luke 10:18.

(I saw) (Satan) (fall) (like) (lightning) (from) (the heights)

Ancient Arabic:

ra'ah   satan   naphal 'aher   baraq   o   bamah.

Jesus said: I saw Satan fall from heaven as baraq o bamah.

The American people and most Christians have no idea what Obama has been doing. Some people who are called the "Tea Party" or the "Patriots" have been crying out for everyone to wake up and take action against him, but what they do not know is that a show of physical power against him is exactly what he is waiting for to prove his point that America needs to be a police state to insure its safety so he can arrest them and put them into prison and began his so called "Act Against Terrorism". The patriot's think back upon the Boston Tea Party and how when they stood up they gained their rights back, but that is not going to work this time because we have entered into the beginning of the Great Tribulation and Satan has been given power over America and God's people.

I just stand in amazement at the things he has been doing and getting away with. A cry rings out inside of me that someone should stop him, but then I know in my spirit that no one can. He is fulfilling Bible prophecy. He is bringing about the "One World Government" and the "Police State" that will implement the "Mark of the Beast. He has been bringing it to pass at a rapid succession and it frankly scares the life out of me! I am a Bible scholar and I know what is happening and what is about to happen shortly to America and to God's people. I want to cry out with the Tea Party, "People of America stop him! Impeach him! Stand up for truth and the America way before it is too late! But then I know inside of my spirit that it is already too late. America has already gone too far. She has already opened up the door for her destruction! We cannot stop it or him. All we can do now is to seek God for our family's protection and the Holy Spirit to guide and protect us through it.

And he cried mightily with a strong voice, saying, "Babylon the great is fallen, is fallen, and is become the habitation of devils, and the hold of every foul spirit, and a cage of every unclean and hateful bird. (Rev.18:2)

America has become the habitation of devils, and the container of every foul spirit.

When I watch the things that are being allowed to happen in America I think "this is really mind boggling that American people would allow this or that!" Some of Obamas laws are just totally insane! Normal people would not allow it! People have to have their minds controlled by devils and demons to go along with Obamas laws and dictates.

People in their right minds just could not do or allow to happen the things that are happening right now and I know most Americans don't even know about them, but keep reading and I will enlighten you to what is going on in your country and what is going to affect your children and your grandchildren.

A law was just passed in California that allows boys to use the same restrooms and get undressed in the same locker rooms as the girls! Now you tell me if that is not insane? This is a real law! It was passed by a real Congress! This is insanity at its greatest! This is demons and devils passing laws and bringing about the devils agenda upon the American children.

I often have said that there is just no way that in America they would ever kill a Christian for not taking the Mark of the Beast, but after seeing this law pass; I now realize that anything can happen in America even the killing of Christians for not being compliant with Obamas laws!

This law was passed to protect homosexuals. If a boy feels like he is a girl, he no longer has to use the boy's bathroom he can use the girls bathroom in any school in California or vice versa if it is a girl.

CALIFORNIA'S TRANSGENDER LAW: California Gov. Brown signs transgender-student bill:

California Gov. Jerry Brown signed a controversial bill into law Monday afternoon allowing the state's transgender public school students to choose which bathrooms they use and whether they participate in boy or girl sports.

The law would cover the state's 6.2 million elementary and high school kids in public schools.

Supporters say the law will help cut down on bullying against transgender students, The families of transgender students have been waging local battles with school districts around the country over what restrooms and locker rooms their children can use.

"Now, every transgender student in California will be able to get up in the morning knowing that when they go to school as their authentic self they will have the same fair chance at success as their classmates," Masen Davis, Executive Director of Transgender Law Center said.

While California is the first state to pass a law of this magnitude, Massachusetts, Connecticut, Washington and Colorado have all adopted policies designed to protect transgendered pupils. Not everyone is on board. Opponents of the bill say allowing students of one gender to use facilities intended for the other could invade the other students' privacy. Randy Thomasson, of savecalifornia.com, says the law would "damage" kids.

"This radical bill warps the gender expectations of children by forcing all California public schools to permit biological boys in girl's restrooms, showers, and clubs and on girls' sports teams and biological girls in boys restrooms, showers, clubs and sports teams," Thomasson said. "This is insanity."

The California bill was backed by a coalition of organizations including Transgender Law Center, Gay-Straight Alliance Network, Gender Spectrum, Equality California, and ACLU of California, National Center for Lesbian Rights and statewide teacher and parent organizations.

3

HABITATION OF DEVILS

And he cried mightily with a strong voice, saying, Babylon the great is fallen, is fallen, and is become the habitation of devils, and the hold of every foul spirit, and a cage of every unclean and hateful bird.

When I think about the children of America and my own grandchildren, my heart just breaks. Without the mercy of God they do not have a chance in the world to grow up without being influenced and controlled by devils. It is and will be all they see and know. It will be natural for them. It is everywhere around them. It is in the school system, on the television and for some growing up in same sex marriage families its right in the home.

America has opened herself up to demons and devils and every foul and evil spirit has possessed her. How did this happen? And when did this happen?

This big change really began during World War II which officially began on September 1, 1939 when Germany invaded Poland. World War II lasted until both the Germans and the Japanese had surrendered to the Allies in 1945.

Women left the home to work in the bomb factories. Women have always worked outside the home but never before in the numbers or with the same impact as they did in World War II. With men off to fight a worldwide war across the Atlantic and the Pacific, women were called to take their place on the production line. The War Manpower Commission, a Federal Agency established to increase the manufacture of war materials, had the task of recruiting women into employment vital to the war effort. Women had proven that they could do the job and within a few decades, women in the workforce became a common sight.

This left the children to be cared for by others without parental control or guidance. The "Latch Key Kids', was created. This gave the children time to get involved in and do things that they should not be doing with no one to watch or stop them. With this open door Satan came in and began to recruit the American children. Many longing for the family unit of security joined gangs and secret groups. They turned to their friends and alienated themselves from their parents.

It used to be that the children had planned schedules. They would get up at dawn to work the family farm. They would feed the animals and till the ground for a garden, mend the fence etc. They would work really hard before and after school. In the evening the family would sit around a nice meal together and the father would read to them out of the Bible. They would all go to church as a family unit on Sundays. The children worked hard. They had rules, guidelines, and boundaries. This created a sense of security and belonging for them and they grew up with good morals and were good people.

Today because of the women working outside of the home as well as the men, they come home and both the mother and the father are so tired that they have very little energy left to give to the kids who are starving for affection and attention. They ponder the kids off to watch TV or to play video games (all of which Satan uses to indoctrinate and intoxicate them).

These same young people growing up in the 60's began to rebel. They rebelled against the war in Viet Nam and the draft and turned from listening to their parents and the government to grouping themselves together in their own little worlds of marijuana, drugs, and free sex.

Their children were called the baby boomers and they grew up having disrespect for any kind of authority because their parents were strung out on drugs and did not discipline them and give them guidance and boundaries.

A spirit of lawlessness and rebellion was released in America. People's love for each other began to grow cold and the "Happy Days" of life in the 50"s was over for America.

The children of America after a few decades of rebellion and doing things their own way have become bored and are now doing unthinkable, ungodly things just because they don't know what else to do with their time.

Two teenagers were charged Tuesday with first-degree murder in the shooting death of a college baseball player out for a jog in Oklahoma — a crime that one teen said they carried out simply because they were bored, according to police.

Oklahoma teens say they shot and killed an Australian baseball player because they were "bored", according to police. James Francis Edwards Jr., 15, and Chancey Allen Luna, 16, were charged with murder. A third teenager, Michael Dewayne Jones, 17, was charged with being an accessory to murder after the fact and with firing a weapon.

Two teens were accused of savagely beating 88-year old WWII Veteran to death. Belton was pronounced dead early Thursday morning after being brutally beaten by the two teens in a parking lot on Wednesday evening. When the teens were questioned they said they did it because they were bored.

In Cincinnati a man was assaulted and robbed by six teens during a "boredom beating" in North College Hill and died. Pat Mahaney, 46, passed away at University of Cincinnati Medical Center a little less than a year after the vicious beating that caused him to suffer internal bleeding and put him in the hospital for four days. Investigators determined the teens instigated the August 2012 attack because they were "bored" and looking for something to do.

Our youth are tired and bored with the TV and the video games. They are going out now looking for a greater thrill and this includes murdering and torturing people and animals.

If they can't find a person to torture or murder they are doing it to dogs and animals. Kids torture dogs and are so brazen about it that they film it and post it on the internet. They twirl them around by their tails then throw them off of 2 story buildings. They hang little puppies by their necks until they are dead. They cut off dog's snouts and break cat's backs. These are the pictures our children can watch on the internet. I just watched a video on the internet of children torturing other children.

The latest game they are playing is called "The knock-out game". This is when a group of boys walk down the street in broad day light, and when they pass an unsuspecting person one of them steps over and throws a deadly punch at the passerby trying to knock them out with one punch. They do not know these people that they are hurting, and there is no motive for hurting them other than they are bored and playing a game! Many people are being killed by this game. It is not safe to pass any teens on the street in broad day light now without being on your guard against attack!

And I say "shame on you America"! Because you turn a deaf ear and close your eyes to this and what is happening with our children! Our children are being driven by evil spirits and it is getting worse and worse! We want to hide our heads in the sand and think that this will never come close to us or our families, and I am here to say to you today. "Wake up!" this is coming to us. It's all around us and it's getting worse by the day.

America's young men are not safe either! I watched a story on the news last night and the parents of two teen agers one a girl and one a boy told the story of their children out on a date and 4 black boys and one girl high jacked them and their car and took them to a house and brutally raped them in every way possible, beat, tortured and killed them.. They put the girl in plastic bags and then into a garbage can to suffocate to death and they set the boy on fire and burnt him to death.

We are living in perilous times!

This know also, that in the last days perilous times shall come. For men shall be lovers of their own selves, covetous, boasters, proud, blasphemers, disobedient to parents, unthankful, unholy, Without natural affection, (gay) trucebreakers, false accusers, incontinent, fierce, despisers of those that are good, (hatred for Christians) Traitors, heady, high minded, lovers of pleasures more than lovers of God; Having a form of godliness, but denying the power thereof: from such turn away (2 Tim.3:1-5)

Television is Satan's greatest way to fill our children with evil spirits and to control their minds and influence them. The shows are made by ungodly people in Hollywood who are demon possessed. The shows get across Satan's propaganda. Even the cartoons are demon inspired.

Television has put into the minds of our children and teenagers that premarital sex is ok and is normal. Almost all of the shows even the so called innocent ones show teens and people going to bed together. This is "normal" to our children now. Almost all of the shows now are including someone who is gay with the connotation that this is a good thing and normal.

Hollywood is definitely influencing and controlling our children's minds. There are not enough good things on television to watch to make it a fit thing to even be in our Christian homes. Our minds have become desensitized to the propaganda, agendas, and influence that television has put into our minds and our children's minds.

On television the other night one time Mickey Mouse sweet, loving, admired girl Miley Cyrus put on a performance that was one of the most raunchy, filthy, dirty, sexual shows that I have ever seen and there was American children sitting watching it. After watching her performance I predict that very soon they will be having sex with animals on stage. Last night in her performance she gave Santa Claus a lap dance. It was vulgar, and disgusting.

The role models for our children come from Hollywood and television and they are demon inspired.

The new finding being taught to our children is that we may be the offspring of Martians. Steven Benner of The Westheimer Institute for Science and Technology in Florida has made known his new finding that evidence is building that Earth life originated on Mars and was brought to this planet aboard a meteorite. An oxidized form of the element molybdenum, which may have been crucial to the origin of life, was likely available on the Red Planet's surface long ago, but unavailable on Earth, said Benner, who presented his findings at the annual Goldschmidt geochemistry conference in Florence, Italy.

The world wants to teach our children to believe in anything except the sovereignty and existence of God.

This is just how crazy our government system has become: A former high school teacher in Montana will only serve 30 days in jail, despite being convicted of raping a 14-year-old girl who later committed suicide.

The sentence was handed down by Judge G. Todd Baugh to Stacey Dean Rambold, 54, who admitted to having sexual relations with Cherice Morales, a then 14-year-old student.

Again my heart just breaks when I think of how far the American culture has fallen into sin and how much our children are all influenced by this ungodly worldly system we call "America".

Satan's first tactic was to try to stop Christianity by persecution and murdering God's people, but when he saw that, that did not work; he changed his tactics and turned to deception.

The conflict in the End-Times will be the battle for truth!

When Jesus was asked to explain to the disciples what they were to look for as a sign of his returning, Jesus' first answer was: Look for deception!

And as he set upon the Mount of Olives, the disciples came unto him privately saying; tell us, when shall these things be? And what shall be the sign of thy coming, and of the end of the world? And Jesus answered and said unto them, Take heed that no man deceive you. For many shall come in my name, saying I am Christ, and shall deceive many. (Matt. 24: 3-4)

We beseech you, brethren, by the coming of our Lord Jesus Christ, and by our gathering together unto him, That ye be not soon shaken in mind, or be troubled, neither by spirit, nor by word, nor by letter as from us, as that the day of Christ is at hand. Let no man deceive you by any means: for that day shall not come, except there come a falling away first. (2 Thess. 2: 1-3)

Now the Spirit speaketh expressly, that in the latter times some shall depart from the faith, giving heed to seducing spirits, and doctrines of devils; (1. Tim. 4:1)

Behold, the days come, saith the Lord God, that I will send a famine in the land, not a famine of bread, nor a thirst for water, but of hearing the words of the Lord. (Amos 8:11)

The danger in the End-Times is the deception of truth.

He will use every kind of evil deception to fool those on their way to destruction, because they refuse to love and accept the truth that would save them. (2 Thess. 2:10 NLT)

Because God's people do not spend enough time fasting, praying, and communing with the Holy Spirit, the things of the flesh begin to appeal to them. The deceptions of Satan are rationalized and begin to make sense to them. They begin to replace the truth of the Bible with Satan's self-indulgent truth.

We are living in dangerous times for the Body of Christ as Satan's last attempt to destroy her is blanketing this world at an unprecedented speed and many are falling into it and being deceived by it.

The Apostle Paul told us that two very important things must happen before Jesus returns. First, he said there would be a great falling away of God's people from the true faith, and second, the Anti-christ would be revealed.

Don't let anyone deceive you in any way, for that day (speaking of the Lord's return) will not come until the rebellion occurs and the man of lawlessness is revealed the man doomed to destruction. (2 Thess. 2:3 NIV)

Don't let anyone deceive you in any way! The true Jesus will not come, until the great falling away happens, and the Anti-christ is revealed to the world.

Paul taught the people that the Lord would not return to earth until a very great falling away happens. This falling away is not a minor falling away, it is a major one. Many, many, many, will be deceived in this last day movement. The great deception will continue until the greatest deception of all occurs, which is the revealing of the Anti-christ.

My heart is burdened this morning as I sit and write this book. My heart is overwhelmed and sad because of what I see coming upon God's people and the world. A very great deception is taking place, and many professing Christians are being deceived and will be deceived by it.

Our Churches are filled with professing Christians who are living in fornication, and partaking of all manner of sin and breaking God's laws without even batting an eye. They indulge in the flesh on one hand they say "Praise the Lord!" and on the other hand they are a lukewarm mixture of Christianity and the world of which Jesus said he will spew them out of his mouth on judgment day.

This great deception of the America Jesus (The Jesus that lets you do whatever you want to do) will so invade the minds and hearts of the people of America that when the Anti-christ appears they will accept him as the true Jesus.

Those who don't accept him, those who are sold out to God and spirit filled will be called "Haters" and "Terrorists" and will be hunted down, put into jails, and killed.

For false messiahs and false prophets will rise up and perform signs and wonders so as to deceive, if possible, even God's chosen ones. (Mark 13:22 NLT)

He performs great signs, so that he even makes fire come down from heaven on the earth in the sight of men. And he deceives those who dwell on the earth by those signs which he was granted to do in the sight of the beast, telling those who dwell on the earth to make an image to the beast who was wounded by the sword and lived. (Rev. 13:13-14 NKJV)

One day he will physically appear to the world and they will accept him and believe that the Jesus of the Bible has returned. This American Jesus will work great miracles all at deceiving the people into worshipping him.

I have come in my Father's name, and you do not receive me; if another comes in his own name, him you will receive. (Jo. 5:43 NKJV)

But there were also false prophets among the people, even as there will be false teachers among you, who will secretly bring in destructive heresies, even denying the Lord who bought them, and bring on themselves swift destruction. And many will follow their destructive ways, because of whom the way of truth will be blasphemed. By covetousness they will exploit you with deceptive words; for a long time their judgment has not been idle, and their destruction does not slumber. (2 Pet. 2:1-3)

..Satan...will go out to deceive the nations... (Rev. 20:7-8 NKJV)

4

THE GREAT TRIBULATION HAS BEGUN

The end of the world as we know it has begun. We are in the beginning stages of the Great Tribulation and the Apocalypse. Just saying those words seems so surreal to me. It reminds me of watching those little men standing on the corner dressed in white robes holding up their signs saying "The end of the world is here!" We all thought they were crazy. Now I am the one saying it!

Oh, how I wish I had a ministry like Joyce Myers and could just speak uplifting, comforting words of encouragement, and prosperity to the Body of Christ so they would love me like they do her. But oh no! God has given me the kind of ministry he gave to Jeremiah the Prophet.

He had a message of judgment that upset the people and they did not want to hear what he had to say. They ended up throwing him into a pit to die. My message is hard as well, who wants to hear "repent, prepare and get ready the Great Tribulation has begun?"

God has called me to be an "End-Time Prophet" to the world. He has called me to inform the Body of Christ about the things that are coming upon this world and to help them get prepared to go through them. The only problem with that is that the world and even the Body of Christ don't want to hear or to believe that things are going to get worse not better.

The Body of Christ has been told for decades that Jesus is coming soon and we say that out of our mouths, but we really do not believe in our hearts that he will return in our lifetimes. The actual thought that he could return in our lifetime scares us to death. It would be the end of the world that we love and hold onto so desperately for something we know very little about. Some of us even get mad and think, "I have worked a lifetime to get the material things that I now have and I want to enjoy them in my older years and you're going to tell me that it's all going to be gone shortly?" And that I am going to lose everything that I have worked so hard for?

Yes, my calling is a hard one! I guess I better give up the idea that everyone is going to want to hear what I have to say. But I have to say it anyway. I have to shout it from the housetops because it's like fire shut up in my bones burning its way out. I must proclaim the message that the Lord Jesus has given me to his people and it is this:

My dearly beloved children, the time has finally arrived and I am going to destroy the ungodly civilization that has been created, drive evil off of the planet, set down my kingdom of righteousness and dwell with you forever.

You will begin to see many things that you have never seen before and I don't want you to be afraid or worried. This is my plan to end the wickedness and to dwell with you again. Don't cling to this world or the things in it. Let them go because I am going to destroy it all. Nothing will stand. I am bringing it all down. I am coming to bring justice to my people and to take away the heartache, sorrow, and pain. I am coming to dwell with you forever.

The sad thing is that the Church has gotten so involved and married into this worldly system that she is not going to want Jesus to destroy it all. Most of the Church will side with the Anti-christ system and fight what Jesus is bringing to pass upon this world. They will try to stop him from tearing down their empires.

Jesus sits and laughs at the great men and women who rule this planet as he watches their plans of grandeur to create a "One World Government, Monetary system, and Religion". They think they are the masters of the universe when it one wave of his hand Jesus is going to tumble it all down.

And in the days of these kings shall the God of heaven set up a kingdom, which shall never be destroyed: and the kingdom shall not be left to other people, but it shall break in pieces and consume all these kingdoms, and it shall stand for ever. (Dan. 2:44)

There is about to be a very great falling away from the old time values and teachings of Jesus Christ. It is happening now all around us. Christians who use to refuse to do or say things are doing them now. They are accepting things that the Church world has always called sin. They have let down their guard and demons and devils have come to fill their heads and hearts with their propaganda, agendas and doctrines.

Please realize, understand, and accept this fact:

The world that we have all known is gone forever! The time of God's clock has finally arrived and everything is going to change. There is no going back. Jesus' plan to end this world has begun. Stop fighting it and learn how to work with God through it to

bring his kingdom down to earth. Learn the heart of Father God and his plans for this End-Time process so you can get into agreement with him.

Everything is now in place. It is only a matter of days until our time on earth begins to dwindle down to zero. The pieces of the puzzle have been put into place:

1.   Israel has once again become a nation after 2500 years.

2.   Jesus told us the generation that witness' that event will be the generation he returns in.

3.   The resurrection of the Roman Empire has occurred with the forming of the European Union. This was prophesied in the book of Daniel to happen in the last days.

4.   A one world government has been put into place with the forming of the United Nations.

5.   The world is divided into 10 regions or Kingdoms with the forming of the Club of Rome out of which the Anti-christ will come to power.

6.   World powers of Russia and China have become strong who are End-Time players.

7.   The surrounding nations of Israel are ripe for the war of Ps. 83. They will storm in to destroy Israel

and she will destroy all of them along with Damascus and then live in a state of peace for a short time making the way for the war of Ez. 38.

8. Russia is now strong enough to come down to destroy Israel with Iran and the Muslim nations as her allies fulfilling the war of Ezek. 38. It will be World War III.

9. *The United States has now fallen under the seduction of the Illuminati and the Anti-christ spirit is in control she has turned from her Christian values and is now the Whore of Babylon turning her back on God and embracing demons and devils.*

10. The United States being in control of the One World Government will take away all the guns of the American people and create a "Police State". Our constitution and freedoms will be eliminated.

11. America is the woman riding upon the back of the beast in Revelation. She is the Whore of Babylon and is in control of the Anti-christ beast movement. She will bring the Mark of the Beast to the American people.

12. The Anti-christ when he comes to power will allow America to control him for a short time, and then

he will bomb New York City and destroy it with fire along with the Vatican.

13.   The Anti-christ will move his headquarters from New York to the Middle East or Europe and eventually to Jerusalem where he will enter the temple and call himself "God".

14.   The days of free enterprise in America are over. Obama being filled with the Anti-christ spirit will continue to pass laws to bring the government in total control over the people.

15.   Tony Blair is being used to deceive the American youth into the "One World Religion" by his "Global Faith Movement: The government will control and brainwash our children to become militants of the state through television, school curriculum (Common Core) and propaganda. The Illuminati will succeed through the United Nations to create a "One World Government, Monetary system, and Religion" that will control the whole world. The United Nations will round us up and make us live in "Sustainable Villages" and take away our land. The United States will be in control of all of it until the actual Anti-christ comes into power then he will cast off the control of America and burn her with fire along with the Vatican and Rome.

16.   The beginning of the Mark of the Beast is being implemented with the passing of Obamas health care

law. It states in it that the government can put in the people an under the skin tracking device. They can also come forcibly into your home promoting the police state. This is the beginning of many laws that will be forced upon the American people.

17.   The Illuminati are using "Mind Control" to create situations where people are using guns to kill other people. This is all the government's plan to step in and eventually take away all of the guns of the American people.

18.   Fema camps and detention facilities have been set up to detain and house the American people.

19.   Obama has created his own army that is separate and above the United States Army. He has created his own military to control the American people and to enforce his ungodly laws. They can come into our homes and haul us away without any search warrants or due process of the law.

20.   The Last Pope has been placed into office: St. Malachy's prophecy concerns the end of the world and is as follows: "In the final persecution of the Holy Roman Church there will reign Peter the Roman, who will feed his flock amid many tribulations, after which the seven-hilled city will be destroyed and the dreadful Judge will judge the people, The End."

Peter the Roman has just been placed into office as Head of the State for the Vatican. His name is Pietro

Parolin and it means in Italian: "Peter the Roman". The Pope has just made his announcement to lay down the Church's strict laws that were against gays, abortion, and divorce opening the door for homosexuals to be welcomed into the Church and for the Roman Catholic Church to be a part of the "One World Religion" and to work alongside of the Anti-christ. .

21.   Jesus spoke about evil rising in Matt. 24:9-14. Many will fall away and there will be great lawlessness... the love of many will grow cold. Many shall be offended, and shall betray one another, and shall hate one another. And many false prophets shall rise, and shall deceive many. And because iniquity shall abound, the love of many shall wax cold. When the transgressors have come to the full a King of Fierce countenance shall stand up among the people.

22.   Satan has successfully deceived the Church into believing in a Pre-Tribulation Rapture and when it does not happen there will be a great falling away of God's people from the faith through discouragement and through not being prepared for coming events. This is the great falling away that the Apostle Paul told us about that would happen right before the Anti-christ enforces the Mark of the Beast.

The following is about to happen:

•The first seal has already been opened. This happened in 2008 when Obama became President. This is a time of conquest by peace and diplomacy on the earth by the Anti-christ spirit gaining control and creating a "One World Government" with no one to stop it and eventually under the direction of a great world leader with extraordinary powers.

•The second seal is war:: This is happening now: There will be many wars including the war of Ps. 83 where all the surrounding nations will fight against Israel and Israel will win and expand her borders and become very wealthy and secure for a time and rebuild her temple.

•The third seal: Economic crash, famine, hunger

•The fourth seal: Disease and global viruses. World War III: The war of Ezekiel 38 and 39... Russia, Iran and others come against Israel...There is a major world war between Islam and the Christian West it occurs over 1/4 of the earth surface. America is damaged but still stands in all of her glory. A police state is declared and extremists are killed which include the born again Christians.

•God judges Russia for coming against Israel, some of Russia's major cities are nuked and some other world cities are nuked by Russia...The nations of the world seeing the intervention acknowledge the existence of the God of Israel....

•A worldwide religious movement develops because of the divine intervention of God for Israel against the northern armies... This unites the religions of the world under the concept that there is one God…A new "Holy" Roman Empire in Europe and part of the Middle East is born.

• The Fascist form of Islam is defeated worldwide by acknowledgment of divine intervention, conquest and/or appeasement and a moderate form of Islam joins with the World Church.

• The worldwide religious movement is the catalyst for a world government. The "One World Government" is set up and has no tolerance for terrorists and rounds up and kills all the extremists who includes the born again Christians.

• The fifth seal is opened: Martyrs killed by Mystery Babylon. Persecution of those who say Jesus is the only way to God… This becomes a major focus because the World Church and the western governments will have no tolerance for religious fundamentalists who oppose an all-inclusive world church and propose that their way is the only way. They will believe these people are a threat to world peace and must be dealt with harshly. There will be many Christian martyrs. It will be mostly those who were deceived into believing in a Pre-Tribulation rapture and did not prepare ahead of time and find God's places of safety and protection to hide in. All these are the beginning of sorrows. Then shall they deliver you up to be afflicted, and shall kill you: and ye shall be hated of all nations for my name's sake time (Matt. 24:8-9)

•The world is divided into 10 regions then the Antichrist rises up and begins his reign. He confirms an existing covenant with Israel and other nations, the covenant is confirmed for seven years ... It is signed on the feast of trumpets (Jewish New Year) ...In the agreement Jerusalem becomes an international city and religious center administered by the world church at Rome.....

•The sixth seal is opened. This is a nuclear holocaust: There is a great earthquake.... The sun becomes darkened and the moon is blood red.... people hide themselves in the caves to get away from the radiation. There is hailstones and fire, contamination of water supply, and the atmosphere darkens.

•The sealing of the 144,000 Jews takes place....The gospel of the coming Jewish kingdom under Jesus is preached by the 144,000 anointed and sealed Jews as a witness to the whole world. They are supernaturally protected through the wrath of the Lamb (the trumpet judgments).

The Church (godly remnant) flees to the mountains and is divinely protected by God. And the woman fled into the wilderness, where she hath a place prepared of God that they should feed her there a thousand two hundred and threescore days. (Rev. 12:6)

•The Jewish Temple is directed to be rebuilt but the Dome of the Rock Mosque will remain in the court of the gentiles.

•The two witnesses also appear at this time and give a 1,260 day testimony...All nations or people who try to harm them are in like manner killed....They will preach a coming Jewish kingdom ruled by Jesus ...There will be no rain in the area for 3 1/2 years...They will dress in sackcloth because they will lament the building of the Jewish temple being prepared for the false Messiah and the judgments that will come when he defiles it... The majority in the world will hate the two witnesses and their message... It is very possible that the two witnesses of God will be portrayed by many as the biblical Antichrist and False Prophet.

•The seventh seal: The container of the 7 trumpets. Hailstones, fire and destruction of a third of the world's vegetation. In Rev. Chapter 8 the opening of the seventh seal leads to the judgment of hailstones and fire. This is a consequence of the nuclear explosion or Revelation 6. The first trumpet judgment shows the effect of nuclear winter Rev.8 verse 7. Hails and fire mingled with blood shows huge balls of hail stones falling from the sky causing fires as they skid on the ground creating life threatening injuries from loss of blood. A third part of vegetation on the earth will be destroyed by the nuclear blast.

•.The second trumpet judgment is an asteroid hitting the ocean.

•The third trumpet judgment: Contamination of a third part of the world's water supply. While the second trumpet judgment is a natural disaster the third one is a manmade one. A great star falling from heaven burning as it were a lamp describes a subsequence of the nuclear war which started in Rev. 6. Here a missile with a nuclear warhead is fired from space into earth. This strikes a third part of the rivers and poison water supply with radioactive materials. Wormwood is the English word for Chernobyl in the Ukraine Bible.

•The fourth trumpet: sounds- Darkness to the sun, moon, and stars due to the dust fallout from the asteroid and meteors. Plus Lunar and Solar Eclipses A third part of the atmosphere darkens. This is the aftermath of the nuclear war that broke out in Rev. 6 and the impact of the asteroid collision.

•The fifth trumpet: Releasing the fallen angels and Satan's son from the Abyss onto the earth Tortures of evil creatures emanating from hell: This is the return of the Nephilim. Jesus said as the days of Noah were so shall the days be when I return. The days of Noah were filled with the Nephilim which were the offspring of demons and humans. They will be stinging locusts like beings that torment men for five months.

•The sixth trumpet: China and the Orient invade the Middle East. This war will be a rebellion of the Orient against the leadership of the West under the Anti-christ. Anti-christ will defeat China and her allies.

•The world leader is killed 42 months after signing the covenant but by the power permitted to Satan he comes to life again. He may duplicate the resurrection of Jesus Christ on the feast of First fruits.

•The risen world leader presents himself as God incarnate. He will enter the rebuilt Jewish temple and stop the animal sacrifices... He will proclaim to have fulfilled the requirement for all sacrifice... He will have an image of himself made to stand in the holy place of the temple showing himself and the world that he is God...The Muslims will totally accept him because he will have the same attributes as Allah.... He also will fulfill the expectations of all religion that in reality worships Satan......Israel for the most part will reject this counterfeit Messiah when he defiles the temple...This Roman Empire leader Antichrist will in turn totally reject Israel and will nullify the seven year agreement with them.

•The faithful Jews who believed the message of the two prophets will flee to the mountains where they will be supernaturally protected by God for 1,260 days

•Demons may come in the form of aliens to present the doctrine of demons...The great deception takes place

(The deceiving demons might say that the Jesus/Jehovah deity is a lesser deity of a controlling hostile alien race that fathered the Jews.

•The Beast (Antichrist) is given power to slay the two prophets after 1,260 days of testimony and judgment at the 6th trumpet judgment of Revelation (the second woe) ... The world rejoices thinking the two prophets of God were really the biblical Antichrist and False Prophet.... They continue to embrace the Beast as God.... A world holiday is declared for one week.... The world population thinks the "new age millennium" has begun and they say peace and safety and send gifts to each other.... They make plans to change the calendar. The last 3 1/2 years begins and the Beast is given authority to rule all nations for 42 months

•The False Prophet appears and demands that all worship this satanic man as God. Jerusalem will be under siege...The World Church, and the Vatican will be destroyed and all who do not worship the risen leader as God will be ordered to be killed

•The Resurrection of the two witnesses takes place after 3 1/2 days in view of the whole world.

•The 666 mark of the beast is enforced worldwide so that no one can buy or sell without it

•Satan is cast out of heaven unto the earth with all his angels

•New York and the Vatican are bombed and destroyed by the Anti-christ and his 10 nation confederacy. Anti-christ will no longer tolerate any other religions except the worship of himself and he will no longer tolerate America or the United Nations ruling over him.

•The seventh trumpet: The Rapture of the Church

•The Father gives Jesus the kingdom ...A pre-wrath gathering of the elect by the angel's takes place which we call the Rapture of the Church. This is the first resurrection. The Saints are taken to heaven where they receive their white robes, crowns, and assigned their rewards. They return with Jesus to earth (30 days later) on white horses to fight the Battle of Armageddon. This occurs on the "last day" of the tribulation period when God says time is not more. After they are taken to heaven God pours out his wrath and destroys the earth.

After this I beheld, and, lo, a great multitude, which no man could number, of all nations, and kindred's, and people, and tongues, stood before the throne, and before the Lamb, clothed with white robes, and palms in their hands; And cried with a loud voice, saying, Salvation to our God which sitteth upon the throne, and unto the Lamb." (Rev.7:9-10) And he said to me, these are they which came out of great tribulation, and have washed their robes, and made them white in the blood of the Lamb. Therefore are they before the throne of God, and serve him day and night in his temple: and he that sitteth on the throne shall dwell among them. They shall hunger no more, neither thirst anymore; neither shall the sun light on them, nor any heat. (Rev. 7:17) for the Lamb which is in the midst of the throne shall feed them, and shall lead them unto living fountains of waters and God shall wipe away all tears from their eyes.(Rev.7:11-17)

•The wrath of Father God is poured out on the world and the kingdom of the Beast in the first six vial judgments of Revelation.

The First Bowl- Sores from the Asteroid and Meteor fall out that touches the skin

The Second Bowl- The oceans become blood red from the meteor dust

The Third Bowl- The rivers and streams also turn blood red from the meteor dust.

The Fourth Bowl- Solar Flares

The Fifth Bowl-Darkness caused from the Solar Flares causing a global CMT and power grid failure

The Sixth Bowl- The demons are released to go and gather all nations to battle to Armageddon.

The Seventh Bowl- Is a Polar Shift and change in the earth's surface. Causing the greatest earthquake the world has ever known along with natural disasters

•Satan and his angels deceive the whole world to gather their armies against Israel and against the (so called) hostile alien deity Jehovah.

•The Kingdom of the Beast is judged at the seventh vial judgment......All the cities of the world also fall.

•The second coming of Jesus in great power and glory with his saints on Yom Kippur...The army of the Beast is judged in the winepress of God...The man of sin and his false prophet are cast alive into the Lake of Fire...Satan is bound for 1,000 years...The sheep and goat judgment to determine who be allowed to go into the Kingdom on earth by how they treated Jesus brethren during the tribulation ...All enemies of Jesus are killed. This happens about 30 days after the Rapture of the Church.

•Satan is loosed to test those on earth who lived through the millennium ... The final rebellion takes place......Satan gathers all nations against Jerusalem and the camps of the saints....Fire comes down from heaven and destroys all who come against anointed Jews of God in Israel

•The second resurrection takes place when God raises and judges all who were not raised in the first resurrection... They will all be judged according to their deeds.

•The Devil and all who follow him are cast into the Lake of Fire.

•A new heaven and a new earth...No more death or suffering...All will know God.

•Eternity with unspeakable blessings.

So the countdown has begun. We who are alive now will see all of these things come to pass in our lifetimes. So knowing these things are about to happen now, and knowing that it is finally God's time to destroy this wicked earth what are we supposed to do now? This is a whole lot of knowledge and it can seem frightening.

The clock has begun ticking to end this world and there is no stopping the events now that are about to happen. The only thing fighting the government or creating a civil war is going to do now is cause the arrest of the American people and a reason to implement Obama's police state.

Jesus said those who live by the sword will die by the sword.

God has pulled back his hand and is allowing the people of this world to embrace the wickedness and darkness that is in their hearts and he's allowing them to do just what their evil minds and imaginations have desired, and that is to create a One World Government where they rule the world and the God of the universe is forced out. He will allow them to do this for a short time, but then he is going to step in and show them who's really in control of this universe as he topples their governments and destroys their manmade gods.

But where do the godly appear in all of this? Well, we really do have a great plan and role to play in all of this. When God sent Moses into Egypt to command the Pharaoh to let his people go and the Pharaoh did not listen to God but kept them in bondage, God sent 10 plaques upon the Land of Egypt to destroy it. Not one plaque fell upon the small portion of Egypt where God's people dwelt. All of Egypt was destroyed but God's people were divinely protected as God destroyed Egypt and set his people free. This is exactly what he is going to do again. God's people who are living holy and righteous before him will be divinely protected while Father God destroys this wicked world and brings freedom to his people.

Satan wants God's people to believe that God is going to whisk them all out of the world in a secret rapture so they will not have to go through this time of tribulation. He wants them to believe this so they will not prepare themselves for the things that are just ahead, and by not being prepared he can step in and destroy them. But let me ask you this, when in the Bible did God ever take the people out of the world? The answer is never! Scripture states over and over again how father God protected his people through trials and problems. He never, ever removed them from the earth to avoid tribulation. God protected the Children of Israel *through* the plagues of Egypt. He protected Noah and his family *through* the flood. God protected Lot by having him *flee into the mountains* before he destroyed Sodom and Gomorrah. Do I need to say anymore?

We are definitely going to be here during the Great Tribulation which is Satan's wrath against the Church. During this time there will basically be three types of Christians:

1.   The first group will be the multitudes of born again, spirit filled Christians who believed the false teaching of a Pre-Tribulation Rapture and did not prepare for themselves and their families and they will be caught by the Anti-christ and beheaded for their faith. They will suffer great persecution and torture and there will be many of them.

2.   The second group will be the same as above however because they were not prepared they will take the Mark of the Beast when they see their children hungry or needing medicines. These are the Christians who live in the soul realm and have never been taught how to crucify the flesh and live in the Holy Spirit. They were taught the false teaching of the Pre-Tribulation Rapture and did not prepare themselves in anyway to be able to withstand persecution or temptation.

3.   The third group of Christians will be those who heed this warning and the warnings of all of God's End-Time Prophets who are crying out now to prepare

and they will be hid away in secret, safety bunkers from the face of evil until Jesus comes back to rapture them to heaven after the tribulation is over and right before God pours his wrath out upon the world and destroys it at the seventh trumpet sound. They are the ones who prepared themselves spiritually, mentally, and physically ahead of time.

We have a great active role to play during this time. We will be the ones praying down the judgments upon the Antichrist's kingdom. We won't be passively hid away not doing anything but we will be the light of the world in the darkest history of mankind. There will be a great harvest of souls because of our preaching and teaching.

So, what do we need to do now?

1. Pray and seek God to lead you to an End-Time Preppers group to have fellowship and to make plans together for safety and provision.

2. Seek God with all of your heart, mind, soul, and strength. Pray for his guidance.

3. Store up food, water, medicines at your home and away at a safety bunker that the Lord leads you to build.

4.   Study God's End-Time plans so you will know exactly the order of coming events so you can be a guide and inspiration to a very confused world.

5.   Get your children out of the public school system

6.   Stay informed on current events

7.   Get out of debt

8.   Move out of New York and surrounding areas

9.   Move away from the coastlines and out of cities

10.   Learn to live off the grid

11.   Learn survival skills

12.   Teach your children, families and friends how to prepare themselves

For those of you who live in the Louisiana area we are starting a Christian Preppers group on Saturday Jan. 4th 2014 so we can join together for support. We will work together here in Louisiana to get prepared and then and we will build an "off the grid" place of safety and provision in the mountains for us all to run to when the grid goes down. We are not a militant group. We will not rely upon our weapons to defend us but upon the Holy Spirit to lead and guide us and the angels of God to protect us.

5

THE WHORE OF BABYLON

There came one of the seven angels which had the seven vials, and talked with me, saying unto me, Come hither; I will shew unto thee the judgment of the great whore that sitteth upon many waters:

With whom the kings of the earth have committed fornication, and the inhabitants of the earth have been made drunk with the wine of her fornication.

So he carried me away in the spirit into the wilderness: and I saw a woman sit upon a scarlet colored beast, full of names of blasphemy, having seven heads and ten horns.

And the woman was arrayed in purple and scarlet color, and decked with gold and precious stones and pearls, having a golden cup in her hand full of abominations and filthiness of her fornication.

And upon her forehead was a name written, Mystery, Babylon the Great, The Mother Of Harlots And Abominations Of The Earth.

And I saw the woman drunken with the blood of the saints, and with the blood of the martyrs of Jesus: and when I saw her, I wondered with great admiration.

And the angel said unto me, wherefore didst thou marvel? I will tell thee the mystery of the woman, and of the beast that carrieth her, which hath the seven heads and ten horns.

The Beast that thou sawest was, and is not; and shall ascend out of the bottomless pit, and go into perdition: and they that dwell on the earth shall wonder, whose names were not written in the book of life from the foundation of the world, when they behold the Beast that was, and is not, and yet is.

And here is the mind which hath wisdom. The seven heads are seven mountains, on which the woman sitteth.

And there are seven kings: five are fallen, and one is, and the other is not yet come; and when he cometh, he must continue a short space.

And the Beast that was, and is not, even he is the eighth, and is of the seven, and goeth into perdition.

And the ten horns which thou sawest are ten kings, which have received no kingdom as yet; but receive power as kings one hour with the Beast.

These have one mind, and shall give their power and strength unto the Beast.

These shall make war with the Lamb, and the Lamb shall overcome them: for he is Lord of Lords, and King of Kings: and they that are with him are called, and chosen, and faithful.

And he saith unto me, the waters which thou sawest, where the whore sitteth, are peoples, and multitudes, and nations, and tongues.

And the ten horns which thou sawest upon the Beast, these shall hate the whore, and shall make her desolate and naked, and shall eat her flesh, and burn her with fire.

For God hath put in their hearts to fulfill his will, and to agree, and give their kingdom unto the Beast, until the words of God shall be fulfilled.

And the woman which thou sawest is that great city, which reigneth over the kings of the earth. (Rev. 17)

First:

There is coming a "Judgment" upon the great whore that sits upon many waters. (Rev. 17:1)

Who or what is this great whore?

And yet they would not hearken unto their judges, but they went a whoring after other gods, and bowed themselves unto them: they turned quickly out of the way which their fathers walked in, obeying the commandments of the LORD; but they did not so. (Jdgs. 2:17)

In God's eyes a "whore" is a nation that once served him and then goes after other gods. He only speaks this way in reference to a nation that once served him and had been faithful to him.

America and ancient Israel are the only two countries dedicated to God when the country officially became a nation.

Like Solomon who dedicated Israel upon the temple mount, George Washington dedicated America to God at Saint Paul's Chapel.

The nation of Rome did not ever serve God, they had many gods and Jehovah God was not one of them. Babylon in Iraq never served God, they served Ishtar and Mardock. Only the nation of America was founded upon and married to the God of Israel. People try to say that the End-Time Babylon is Rome or the country of Babylon in Iraq and neither of them fit the description here.

The destruction of the "Great City" of Babylon occurs suddenly, without warning, and when she is at the height of her power destruction comes in one hour. She is burned with fire.

America will ride the back of the Beast system and control it through the United Nations until about the middle of the Tribulation period. She will along with the rest of the world enforce the Mark of the Beast and the killing of Jews and Christians until the blood of the Christians runs so deep within her that God has had enough, then he will put into the hearts of the 10 Kings who support the Anti-Christ to rise up and bomb her and completely destroy New York City in one hour along with disabling the rest of America. Then the Anti-Christ will rise up and rule the world for the last 3 ½ years with nobody else to control or stop him.

The kings of the earth are not expecting this to happen. They stand afar off and are in amazement over the cities destruction.

America is the great whore of Babylon. She sits upon many waters. Waters represents nations. She influences the world.

The Bible tells us that the woman is a city. This can be none other than New York City. *The woman is that great City that rules over the kings of the earth (Rev. 17:18).*

She is sitting upon a scarlet colored beast that had seven heads and ten horns. The Bible tells us the seven heads are seven mountains, contrary to the false teaching that these seven mountains are actually the ‧ Seven Hills of Rome. Mountains always mean countries or nations in the Bible. The Bible says there are seven mountains and these seven mountains or countries each have a king as there are seven kings as well. Five had fallen during John's day.

1) Egypt

2) Assyria

3) Babylon

4) Medo-Persia

5) Grecia

6) Rome - Pagan and Papal - "AND ONE IS" - John lived in the time of this "one is" - Rome

7) U. S. A. - Rome in Europe persecuting and USA in the west.

8) The Beast - Rome "Even he is the eighth, and is of made up of the seven.

America is the Great Whore that is riding upon the back of the Anti-Christ Beast system. She is in control of it in the beginning. The 10 Kings arise that will hate her and bomb her causing Islam and the Anti-Christ's Kingdom to rule supreme.

These 10 kings will bomb the rest of the United States rendering her incapacitated. God will destroy the Babylon in Iraq after the Anti-christ moves his office there near the end of the tribulation period before he moves it on to Jerusalem.

Why does God judge her so strongly? Because in verse 6 it says: And I saw the woman drunken with the blood of the saints, and with the blood of the martyrs of Jesus: and when I saw her, I wondered with great admiration. God is going to avenge her mightily for hurting his children.

You might say this cannot possibly be America as she has never killed any Christians. --- Not yet any way! But she will!

6

MYSTERY BABYLON THE ONE WORLD RELIGION

Mystery Babylon is the world trying to be spiritual without the Holy Spirit. So, what happens first? What End-Time event should I be looking out for next, you might ask. It is the great "Apostasy". It will be a great End-Time deception. It will look like the right thing but it will be fueled by the demons of hell. The world will be lulled into its deceptive ways and from out of it will spring the Anti-christ.

The Apostle Paul said, first will be the Great Apostasy, then the Anti-christ will be revealed. (2 Thess. 2:3)

It is already at work in the world today. It is the New Age Movement of humanitarian good works which includes feeding the hungry, serving people in need, and reaching out a helping hand, and accepting gays and people no matter how they live or what they do. A lot of the movie stars in Hollywood are doing this today. They are doing acts that seem godly and spiritual on the outside, but they are full of sin on the inside. It is the world trying to be spiritual without the Holy Spirit. The Anti-christ will rise from this movement of love and humanitarian benevolence.

Since they thought it foolish to acknowledge God, he abandoned them to their foolish thinking and let them do things that should never be done. (Rom 1:28 NLT)

Movie stars live together in sin, partake of all kinds of sexual sins, take illegal drugs, get drunk, lie, steal, and cheat, yet you see them on television and in the newspapers as "Envoys of Goodwill", and many of them represent our nation to the other nations of the world.

There will be a very great falling away from the "old time religion" that we have all been taught into a belief system that does not have any absolutes. People want to do what they want to do and live how they want to live, but they also want to think that they are spiritual and full of love and good.

The Apostle Paul taught that the second coming of Christ for his Church would not happen until two things happened first. The great falling away or Apostasy from the true faith, and the man of sin or the Anti-christ was revealed.

Let no man deceive you by any means: for that day shall not come, (the rapture) except there come a falling away first, and that man of sin be revealed, the son of perdition. (2 Thess. 2:3)

"Mystery Babylon "is a one world religious system. This one world religious system will rise up and rule the world. It will be a combining of all the religions in the world.

It will be based upon humanism. There will be no absolutes and anything goes. Anything that is, except the teachings of Jesus Christ! The words of Jesus Christ have absolutes, and the world will cast his teachings off and begin to persecute everyone who teaches them and abides by them.

Tony Blair has developed the "Tony Blair Faith Foundation" trying to form a one world religion. He is having much luck. People are falling into the web of deception by the thousands. He is combining people of all faiths into a one world religion. He along with several well-known individuals are swooning the world into a religion of faith and spirituality without any absolutes or Holy Spirit.

Mystery Babylon is a false religion and is being taught to the world by many of its prominent leaders. A great wave of teachings that emphasize spirituality without the absolutes of Jesus Christ is sweeping our nation.

Ophra Winfrey said that there are many ways to God, and that you do not have to go through Jesus

Christ to get there. She also endorses the fact that being gay is a gift from God. Obama teaches the same thing. I guess it is no wonder that she backs him in his Presidency.

Dr. Wayne Dyer is a motivational speaker and has influenced thousands of Americans with his teachings. He teaches it is possible for every person to manifest their deepest desires — if they honor their inner divinity, consciously choose to live from their "Highest Self."

He teaches the New Age Movement that it is the Self that saves us, and thousands have been deceived by his teachings.

Great persecution is what's coming next for anyone who truly follows Jesus Christ, and my heart breaks because we have not been taught how to be prepared for this great persecution.

We will be hunted down and put into prisons and camps. Churches will be closed down, and anyone who preaches from their pulpits the absolutes of Christ will be arrested. You will no longer be able to make any statement regarding homosexuality as being a sin, or any other form of sin.

Marriage between people of the same sex will be legalized everywhere.

Mystery Babylon will not tolerate any absolutes! The teachings that will rule the world is the love of "self". If you have a Facebook account you can already hear the teachings of a lot of people voicing this message. They are stating for the born again Christians to stop being haters and to embrace the gay lifestyle.

It will be the exact opposite of the teachings of Christ. Christ taught to crucify and deny the self. Mystery Babylon will teach to love the self and to exalt it above all. It will be the spirit of Satan that cried out "I will! Exalt my throne above the stars of God! (Isa. 14:13).

It will be the "I will!" not the "Thy will" that will be the order of the day.

Born again Christians will be hated by all nations. We will be called, the haters and the terrorists.

"Then you will be handed over to be persecuted and put to death, and you will be hated by all nations because of me. (Matt. 24:9 NIV)

If you belonged to the world, it would love you as its own. As it is, you do not belong to the world, but I have chosen you out of the world. That is why the world hates you. (John 15:19 NIV)

Woe to you Christian, if you find yourself totally fitting into the world and its systems. If you are then something is terribly wrong with your Christian walk! In these end-times the closer you get to Jesus the more the world will hate you not love you!

This persecution has already begun and Mystery Babylon has been rising for some time now. Our great motivational speakers and leaders have all been guiding us into this one world religion for years.

Mystery Babylon is the one world false religion including the Roman Catholic Church.

Mystery Babylon received its name because of its origin. The "Mystery" about Babylon is the magical arts, and devil worship that went on in secret by the priests of ancient Babylon. They were able to open a portal to the underworld and make contact with Lucifer and his demons that spoke to them and gave them special powers. They did this by building a very tall tower that ascended up into the sky. They worshipped the host of the underworld on the top of this tower. They had developed a "Star gate" on the top of the tower through which demons and devils could come through.

God the Father came down to see what they were doing and was very displeased. He scattered the people all over the world by changing their languages so they could not understand one another. Those who spoke the same language all went off to start new cities elsewhere. Therefore the tower was left empty.

God had told the people to scatter on the face of the earth, but they had disobeyed him and all gathered in one place and through the power of Lucifer established a one world government, religion, and monetary system. Their ruler was Nimrod, a servant of Lucifer.

Nimrod ruled the Kingdom of Babylon and the first great rebellion against God and the host of heaven was established. Babylon was the mother of harlots and the abominations of the world! This false religion has spread all over the earth.

One day very soon the Demon King of the Abyss will be unleashed upon this world and he will rule it, right now he is being restrained in the bottomless pit. (Rev. 9:11)

The beast you saw was once alive but isn't now. And yet he will soon come up out of the bottomless pit and go to eternal destruction. And the people who belong to this world, whose names were not written in the Book of Life before the world was made, will be amazed at the reappearance of this beast who had died. (Rev: 17:8NLT)

The Anti-christ will come in as a man of peace. He will rule for 3 1/2 years and then be assassinated by a sword wound to the head. When he dies the demon king from the Abyss which will be given power by Satan will be released from the Abyss by the angel of God and will enter his body and rule the world for 3 ½ years.

He will confirm a 7 year peace plan with many people. The Jews will rebuild their temple and the sacrifices will be resumed. He will enter their temple and proclaim himself as God. He will receive his power and authority from Lucifer his father. He will persecute and kill the Jews and all Christians that he can capture.

When the angel spoke to the Apostle John on the isle of Patmos when he gave him the book of Revelation, Jesus said, that Satan's throne was on this earth in the town of Pergamos. The high priests with their magical arts had gone to Pergamos after the Tower of Babel was destroyed by God.

When Pergamos was conquered and defeated the priests fled to Rome and took up their residence in the Vatican. Satan's seat was moved to Rome. This same devil worship has moved to the United States and can be found in the prayer room at the United Nations building. So Babylon, the seat of Satan, moved to Rome, then to the United States making the United States the End-Time Babylon of the Bible. There are three Babylon's spoken of in scriptures. The Economic Babylon is New York and the United States that will be destroyed by atomic bombs in one hour. The second Babylon is the physical one that is located in Iraq. God will destroy this one near the end of the Great Tribulation. It will be the headquarters of the Anti-christ. The third Babylon is "Mystery Babylon" which is the one world religion.

The black priests in Rome practice demon and devil worship in secret and perform all the magical arts from ancient Babylon. A pope will arise from there that is knowledgeable in these arts and he will turn the papacy to worship the Anti-christ, causing a major split, between the deceived ones and the godly ones.

Every year the United States President and the most powerful men in the world meet at the Bohemian Grove campground in Monte Rio, California. It is a

2,700 acre campground where they spend 2 weeks and 3 weekends having occult ceremonies outside under a giant 40 foot owl.

Therefore God's wrath against the Vatican and Rome is great due to all of God's innocent children that they have caused to suffer and killed over the years, and due to some of the evil Popes who have reigned, but his wrath is also against America because she was founded upon biblical principles but has turned from God to worship demons and devils.

Some think that the ancient city of Babylon must be rebuilt to its former glory before the Tribulation can begin because of the scriptures that say that it will be destroyed without inhabitant and that has not happened yet. And it's true that it hasn't happened yet. But it will not be built back to its former glory which would take years before the Lord Jesus returns and then it could never possess all of the characteristics that the Bible describes the End-Time Babylon would have. It could never be a deep sea port city.

The End-Time Mystery Babylon the Bible speaks about is a system of devil worship that originated in ancient Babylon and has spread to Rome, to the United States, the United Nations, and the EU, and it is ruling this world in these last days. It will grow stronger and stronger until it controls every nation under a one world dictator.

So, get ready saints, get prepared you children of the great king, and be about your Fathers business, because the Lord Jesus is coming back in this generation!

So, what should we do now to prepare for Mystery Babylon rising? We need to begin to live off the grid as much as possible. Born again Christians will begin to lose their jobs as the persecution becomes stronger, so if at all possible become self-employed.

Buy a piece of land and begin to cultivate and grow your own food. Stock up on supplies of all kinds now. Buy gold or silver or have some other commodity to barter with. If you can't afford to buy a piece of land in the country for yourself, then join with the rest of your family and relatives and all pitch in to get some land. Move out of the cities!

Find other born again Christians who have the understanding of these things and join up with them for mutual support, to share commodities and to develop a Christian Community.

Begin to study and teach others how to be encouraged when they find themselves arrested and put in prison and how to trust God through it so their faith does not fail.

7

THE FALL OF BABYLON

The one world religion was a tool used by Satan to turn the people of the earth away from the absolutes of the Bible to self-indulgence. It would have been too great a jump for Satan to deceive people to go from the absolutes of the Bible straight to Satan worship.

Mystery Babylon was only Satan's tool to begin to deceive the world. He allowed them all to be pulled into the web of self-love and humanism, and he tolerated them worshipping their own selves instead of him but after the first three and a half years of the Great Tribulation when the Anti-christ reveals himself as God and desires to be worshipped, the Anti-christ won't tolerate any worship other than his own, the False Prophet will join with the Anti-christ and will destroy Rome, the Vatican , America and the Mystery Babylon religion and set up the worship of his own self.

The False Prophet will use his influence over all the people to switch the worship to the Anti-christ and make everyone take a mark on their right hand or forehead symbolizing their allegiance to him.

And after these things I saw another angel come down from heaven, having great power; and the earth was lightened with his glory.

And he cried mightily with a strong voice, saying, Babylon the great is fallen, is fallen, and is become the habitation of devils, and the hold of every foul spirit, and a cage of every unclean and hateful bird.

For all nations have drunk of the wine of the wrath of her fornication, and the kings of the earth have committed fornication with her, and the merchants of the earth are waxed rich through the abundance of her delicacies.

And I heard another voice from heaven, saying, Come out of her, my people, that ye be not partakers of her sins, and that ye receive not of her plagues.

For her sins have reached unto heaven and God hath remembered her iniquities.

Reward her even as she rewarded you, and double unto her double according to her works: in the cup which she hath filled fill to her double.

How much she hath glorified herself, and lived deliciously, so much torment and sorrow give her: for she saith in her heart, I sit a queen, and am no widow, and shall see no sorrow.

Therefore shall her plagues come in one day, death, and mourning, and famine; and she shall be utterly burned with fire: for strong is the Lord God who judges her.

And the kings of the earth, who have committed fornication and lived deliciously with her, shall bewail her, and lament for her, when they shall see the smoke of her burning,

Standing afar off for the fear of her torment, saying, alas, alas that great city Babylon, that mighty city! For in one hour is thy judgment come.

New York (Babylon) will be destroyed in one hour. The Vatican and Rome will also be destroyed. God's judgment will fall heavily upon the earthly seat of Satan which is the Vatican, and New York.

Ancient Babylonian devil worship was transferred from Pergamos to the Vatican and in secret the high priests have continued the Satanic worship that began in ancient Babylon and has spread all over the earth.

With the one world religion gone, the only religion that will be tolerated upon the earth will be the worship of the Anti-christ.

The beast and the ten horns you saw will hate the prostitute. They will bring her to ruin and leave her naked; they will eat her flesh and burn her with fire. (Rev. 17:16 NIV)

God in his mercy calls for every true believer to come out of the false one world religious system and return to him so they will not be destroyed with her destruction. He also sends out a warning to Rome and New York prior to their destruction warning all Christians to flee the cities.

8

THE ILLUMINATI

There really is a great cover-up. There really is a conspiracy, and the agenda is two-fold. The goal is to create a one world government, monetary system, and religion and at the same time drive every born again Christian off the face of the earth.

Satan is preparing the world for his take over, and he has people doing his bidding behind the scenes to bring this to pass.

There are men and women of great wealth, and power that are and have been working behind the scenes to accomplish this goal. Their leader is Lucifer. They believe they are the "Illuminated Ones", who hold earth's hidden knowledge and wisdom. They believe it is their duty to bring about these changes upon the earth.

We don't see them at work; we only see their ponds that are on the forefront, such as Obama. These people are all working together behind the scenes and they are the real ones who put in presidents and leaders all over the country and who are making all of the important decisions. They are making the decisions that bring us closer to a universal one world government.

Lucifer has blinded their minds and made them believe that they are doing the world good and that the world needs their leadership. They do not believe that people are capable of ruling this planet on their own.

What they do to accomplish their goals is very smart on one hand, but very wrong and cruel on the other hand. They cause situations to happen so they can rise up and further their cause.

During times of national crisis the government is entrusted with the authority to implement any and all means necessary to secure the safety of the people. Knowing this they create these national crisis.

World War II ended 5/7/1945 and the United Nations was born on 10/24/1945. The Illuminati created and used this war to take the world one step closer to a one world government.

The twin towers were destroyed on 9/11/2001, one month later the USA Patriot Act was redesigned to take away a lot of our constitutional rights and it was passed. The Illuminati created and used this terrible event to further the one world government.

This Patriot Act tramples upon our constitutional rights. It violates the Fourth Amendment, which requires government to show probable cause before obtaining a search warrant. Second, the act violates the First Amendment by imposing a gag order on public employees required to provide government with their clients' personal information. The act also violates the First Amendment by effectively authorizing the FBI to investigate American citizens for, in part, exercising their freedom of speech and, it eliminates the requirement for government to provide notice to individuals whose privacy has been compromised by a government investigation.

The government is now free to come into our homes and search and seize without a search warrant. They also have the power to execute us on the spot if we resist.

This law removes our "due process' which we are entitled to under the Constitution, and gives the government judicial process which means they can come in and kill us without any procedure first.

The US can kill any opponents of Obama. The US can now legally kill any group that they deem is a terrorist group without any due process of law.

When the U.S. government claims the power to target and kill American citizens in the fight against terrorists its serious business. This means that if you are in a church where the pastor is preaching against homosexuals the government can come in and kill everyone legally.

In the boldest admission yet that the Obama administration intends the extra-judicial execution of American citizens; Director of National Intelligence Dennis Blair confirmed on Wednesday that the U.S. intelligence community is authorized to assassinate Americans abroad who are considered direct terrorist threats to the United States.

This places President Obama in clear and direct violation of his Oath of Office to "uphold, protect and defend the Constitution of the United States," the duty which overrides all other duties of the president. *This is the first time a US president has asserted the right to murder any American citizen upon an executive order.*

The assertion of power relies on the post-9/11 claim that "the entire world" is now the battlefield, including the United States, and that "targets" may be killed at any time; as they sleep, dine, or travel, and not just during the heat of an actual battle.

January 1 of this year President Obama signed into law the NDAA (National Defense Authorization Act).

The most chilling aspect of NDAA was the indefinite detention of US citizens who were only assumed to be tied to terrorist organizations.

Never mind the fact that our own government has been in bed with these same terrorists and continue to fund them. A good example is the recent take-over of Libya and execution of Gaddafi.

The thing that is so amazing is that the American people are more concerned about how much they pay for gas, than they are about their God given rights being trampled upon.

The NDAA is in effect stating that the government can merely say you are a terrorist or affiliated with terrorists and can ship you off to anywhere in the world to be detained and even tortured at its discretion without proof and without due process, which you are supposed to be guaranteed under the Constitution.

Just this month it became even more alarming as in a 60 minutes interview, Secretary of Defense Leon Panetta acknowledged the US has the authority to assassinate those they deem to be terrorists with no arrest, no jury, and no trial.

What is the Federal Emergency Management Agency? Simply put, it is the "secret government". This agency has powers and authority that go well beyond any other agency in the nation.

What can FEMA do? It can suspend laws. It can move entire populations. It can arrest and detain citizens without a warrant and can hold them without a trial. It can seize property, food supplies, and transportation systems. And it can even suspend the Constitution of the United States.

A Halliburton subsidiary has just received a $385 million contract from the Department of Homeland Security to provide "temporary detention and processing capabilities."

There over 800 prison camps in the United States, all fully operational and ready to receive prisoners. They are all staffed and even surrounded by full-time guards, but they are all empty. These camps are to be operated by FEMA (Federal Emergency Management Agency) should Martial Law need to be implemented in the United States and all it would take is a presidential signature on a proclamation and the attorney general's signature on a warrant to which a list of names is attached.

The camps all have railroad facilities as well as roads leading to and from the detention facilities. Many also have an airport nearby. The majority of the camps can house a population of 20,000 prisoners. Currently, the largest of these facilities is just outside of Fairbanks, Alaska. The Alaskan facility is a massive mental health facility and can hold approximately 2 million people.

After 9/11, new martial law plans began to surface similar to those of FEMA in the 1980s. In January 2002, the Pentagon submitted a proposal for deploying troops on American streets. One month later, John Brinkerhoff, the author of the 1982 FEMA memo, published an article arguing for the legality of using U.S. troops for purposes of domestic security.

The following are Executive Orders associated with FEMA that would suspend the Constitution and the Bill of Rights. These Executive Orders have been on record for nearly 30 years and could be enacted by the stroke of a Presidential pen:

EXECUTIVE ORDER 10990

Allows the government to take over all modes of transportation and control of highways and seaports.

EXECUTIVE ORDER 10995

Allows the government to seize and control the communication media.

EXECUTIVE ORDER 10997

Allows the government to take over all electrical power, gas, petroleum, fuels and minerals.

EXECUTIVE ORDER 10998

Allows the government to seize all means of transportation, including personal cars, trucks or vehicles of any kind and total control over all highways, seaports, and waterways.

EXECUTIVE ORDER 10999

Allows the government to take over all food resources and farms.

EXECUTIVE ORDER 11000

Allows the government to mobilize civilians into work brigades under government supervision.

EXECUTIVE ORDER 11001

Allows the government to take over all health, education and welfare functions.

EXECUTIVE ORDER 11002

Designates the Postmaster General to operate a national registration of all persons.

EXECUTIVE ORDER 11003 allows the government to take over all airports and aircraft, including commercial aircraft.

EXECUTIVE ORDER 11004 allows the Housing and Finance Authority to relocate communities, build new housing with public funds, designate areas to be abandoned, and establish new locations for populations.

EXECUTIVE ORDER 11005

Allows the government to take over railroads, inland waterways and public storage facilities.

EXECUTIVE ORDER 11051

Specifies the responsibility of the Office of Emergency Planning and gives authorization to put all Executive Orders into effect in times of increased international tensions and economic or financial crisis.

EXECUTIVE ORDER 11310

Grants authority to the Department of Justice to enforce the plans set out in Executive Orders, to institute industrial support, to establish judicial and legislative liaison, to control all aliens, to operate penal and correctional institutions, and to advise and assist the President.

EXECUTIVE ORDER 11049

Assigns emergency preparedness function to federal departments and agencies, consolidating 21 operative Executive Orders issued over a fifteen year period.

EXECUTIVE ORDER 11921

Allows the Federal Emergency Preparedness Agency to develop plans to establish control over the mechanisms of production and distribution, of energy sources, wages, salaries, credit and the flow of money in U.S. financial institution in any undefined national emergency. It also provides that when a state of emergency is declared by the President, Congress cannot review the action for six months. The Federal Emergency Management Agency has broad powers in every aspect of the nation.

General Frank Salzedo, chief of FEMA'S Civil Security Division stated in a 1983 conference that he saw FEMA'S role as a "new frontier in the protection of individual and governmental leaders from assassination, and of civil and military installations from sabotage and/or attack, as well as prevention of dissident groups from gaining access to U.S. opinion, or a global audience in times of crisis."

FEMA's powers were consolidated by President Carter to incorporate the...

National Security Act of 1947

Allows for the strategic relocation of industries, services, government and other essential economic activities, and to rationalize the requirements for manpower, resources and production facilities.

1950 Defense Production Act

Gives the President sweeping powers over all aspects of the economy.

Act of August 29, 1916

Authorizes the Secretary of the Army, in time of war, to take possession of any transportation system for transporting troops, material, or any other purpose related to the emergency.

International Emergency Economic Powers Act

Enables the President to seize the property of a foreign country or national. These powers were transferred to FEMA in a sweeping consolidation in 1979.

Obama has turned America from a free Republic into a Fascist Tyranny. He has removed some of our God given constitutional rights and continues to do so, and set himself up in a position to kill us if he doesn't like something we say or believe in.

Obama signed into law in 2009 the Hate Crime Law which states that speaking out against homosexuals or any group is punishable by law. It makes it a federal crime to speak out against someone's sexual orientation or gender identity.

Obama continues to take away the Christians rights to free speech regarding the Bible's stand against sin.

He is taking away our rights to free speech, along with some of our most important Constitutional rights as American citizens by the Hate Law bill and the Patriot Act law.

It is now against the law to preach homosexuality is a sin from our pulpits. It's just a matter of time before Obama begins to enforce this law by hauling our pastors to jail.

Obama passed a recent law that removes our Freedom of Speech. The law states that if a group rally is being held that he can send forces in and declare that it is off limits and the person or meeting must be dissolved, and if it is not they can detain or kill you. The HR 347 law makes our public protesting against the law.

President Obama signed into law the Federal Restricted Buildings and Grounds Improvement Act of 2011. This law permits Secret Service agents to designate any place they wish as a place where free speech, association and petition of the government are prohibited and it permits the Secret Service to make these determinations based on the content of speech.

Thus, federal agents whose work is to protect public officials and their friends may prohibit the speech and the gatherings of folks who disagree with those officials or permit the speech and the gatherings of those who would praise them, even though the First Amendment condemns content-based speech discrimination by the government. The new law also provides that anyone who gathers in a "restricted" area may be prosecuted and because the statute does not require the government to prove intent, a person accidentally in a restricted area can be charged and prosecuted, as well.

He is passing laws that take away our rights under the Constitution and Bill of Rights.

Now the authorities can "strip search you for minor offenses!

It might seem that in the United States, being pulled over for driving without a seat belt should not end with the government ordering you to take off your clothes and "lift your genitals." But there is no guarantee that this is the case -- not since the Supreme Court ruled this week that the Constitution does not prohibit the

114

government from strip searching people charged with even minor offenses.

The court's 5-4 ruling turns a deeply humiliating procedure -- one most Americans would very much like to avoid -- into a routine law enforcement tactic. But the Supreme Court, by a 5-4, has now given its blessing to strip searches of people who are charged with minor crimes -- even if the government has no specific reason to believe they are concealing anything.

And the list goes on, and on, and on. The Illuminati is running this world and they are Satan's servants. They are the power people behind the scenes that are bringing Satan's plans and purposes to pass on this earth. They are creating crisis so they can they step in and create a new law to further their cause and gain more control of the world.

We as American people have had our constitution compromised right under our noses. Many of our constitutional rights have been removed and *Obama now has full legal right to arrest, detain us, and search and seize our belongings and even kill us without a fair trial.*

He has made the laws regarding our freedom of speech a hate crime. His next agenda is to begin his prosecution of the born again Christians and close up our churches. We will be hunted down and arrested for speaking and preaching the Bible truths.

We are about to enter into a time of great persecution and martyrdom for our faith. The true Christians will get in all the way, and the lukewarm ones will fall away.

Obama also hates Israel. He has been trying to get them to give up their land and to retract their borders back to the pre-1967 borders. This is an outrage to peace, sovereignty of Israel, and a stable Middle East," former Arkansas Gov. Mike Huckabee (R), a 2008 Republican presidential candidate who's been a staunch supporter of Israel, said in a statement:

When a nation becomes anti-Israel that country loses God's blessing.

These laws are not something that might happen in our future. They are laws that Obama has already placed into effect. The only thing now that we have to look forward to in the future is a certain enforcing of them by him. It's just a matter of time.

Obama wants us to sit quietly by while he passes laws and changes America into a Socialist nation, and he is succeeding right under our noses.

Obama's statement to the Supreme Court was just taken by some as a threat, that they better approve his Obama-Care package. He is even trying to rule our Supreme Court!

Do you realize his health care program will demand we carry health insurance? This takes away our rights. He keeps passing laws and little by little, one law at a time our constitutional rights are being removed and he set himself up as a dictator.

Obama Care has a microchip implant for you... The Obama Health care bill includes (under Class II, Paragraph 1, Section B) "(ii) a class II device that is implantable". Then on page 1004 it describes what the term "data" means in paragraph 1, section B: It does not say it is mandatory for everyone, however it is only the first step.

His health care package demands everyone to carry health insurance and it opens the door up for everyone to receive a microchip implant before they can receive health care. This is one step forward towards receiving the Mark of the Beast before you can buy or sale:

So that no one could buy or sell unless he had the mark, which is the name of the beast or the number of his name. (Rev. 13:17)

Everything he is going about doing is ending up removing our rights under the Constitution of the United States. He is determined to change the constitution to meet his own agendas.

And he (the antichrist) will try to change the set times and the laws. (Dan. 7:25)

The Patient Protection and Affordable Care Act, known as Obama-Care was passed by Congress on

March 21, 2010, and signed into federal law by President Barack Obama on March 23. This law began the process to socialize the United States health care.

The centerpiece of Obama Care is the individual mandate, a provision that makes it mandatory for every citizen to purchase private health insurance, which is unprecedented in American history.

So, what do we do now? We make sure we hear from God as to where we are to have a secret place of refuge and make sure that place is prepared ahead of time.

They are coming after us Saints! It's here! The Great Tribulation is upon us and there is no turning it back. The next thing Obama will do is to take away the guns of the American people so we can't defend ourselves against the government. Watch for this, it's coming!

9

AGENDA 21

Agenda 21 is the United Nations Agenda for the 21st Century. The United Nations who are made up of the council of 300 and the Illuminati who are the wealthy puppeteers who rule this world have decided that people are destroying the planet and they have come up with their own agenda to stop the worlds destruction by implementing new rules and regulations for everyone to abide by which have been signed into law and every nation has agreed to abide by them including the United States.

They don't tell us about their goals and agendas, they just secretly put them into force under our noses with the America people oblivious to what's really happening all around them and to what is being implemented that will drastically affect their lives.

In a nutshell, the plan calls for governments to take control of all land use and not leave any of the decision making in the hands of private property owners. It is assumed that people are not good stewards of their land and the government will do a better job if they are in control.

Individual rights in general are to give way to the needs of communities as determined by the governing body.

Moreover, people should be rounded up off the land and packed into human settlements, or islands of human habitation, close to employment centers and transportation.

Another program, called the Wildlands Project spells out how most of the land is to be set aside for non-humans.

"The current life styles and consumption patterns of the affluent middle class- involving high meat intake, the use of fossil fuels, electrical appliances, home and work place air conditioning, and suburban housing, -are not sustainable."

"Effective execution of Agenda 21 will require a profound reorientation of all human society, unlike anything the world has ever experienced a major shift in the priorities of both governments and individuals and an unprecedented redeployment of human and financial resources."

This shift will demand that a concern for the environmental consequences of every human action be integrated into individual and collective decision-making at every level.

- Excerpt, UN Agenda 21

UN Agenda 21/Sustainable Development is the action plan implemented worldwide to inventory and control all land, all water, all minerals, all plants, all animals, all construction, all means of production, all energy, all education, all information, and all human beings in the world. *(In other words, the Illuminati are going to take over our lives and run things because we are too stupid to do it for ourselves and sustain the planet).*

Have you wondered where these terms 'sustainability' and 'smart growth' and 'high density urban mixed use development' came from? Doesn't it seem like about 10 years ago you'd never heard of them and now everything seems to include these concepts? Is that just a coincidence? That every town and county and state and nation in the world would be changing their land use/planning codes and government policies to align themselves with...what?

First, before I get going, I want to say that yes, I know it's a small world and it takes a village and we're all one planet etc. So I'm not against making certain issues a priority, such as mindful energy use, alternative energy sponsorship, recycling/reuse, and sensitivity to all living creatures.

But then you have UN Agenda 21. What is it?

Agenda 21 – The UN Blueprint for the 21st Century:

Agenda 21 was the main outcome of the United Nation's Earth Summit held in Rio de Janeiro in 1992. Agenda 21 outlines, in detail,

The UN's vision is for a centrally managed global society. This contract binds governments around the world to the United Nation's plan for controlling the way we live, eat, learn, move and communicate - all under the noble banner of saving the earth. When fully implemented, Agenda 21 would have the government involved in every aspect of life of every human on earth. (This is how the Mark of the Beast will be implemented).

Agenda 21 spreads it tentacles from Governments, to federal and local authorities, and right down to community groups. Chapter 28 of Agenda 21 specifically calls for each community to formulate its own Local Agenda 21: Each local authority should enter into a dialogue with its citizens, local organizations, and private enterprises to formulate 'a Local Agenda 21.' Through consultation and consensus-building, local authorities would learn from citizens and from local, civic, community, business and industrial organizations and acquire the information needed for formulating the best strategies." - Agenda 21, Chapter 28, sec 1.3

At the summit 179 nations officially signed Agenda 21 and many more have followed since. Nearly 12,000 local and federal authorities have legally committed themselves to the Agenda.

In practice this means that all their plans and policies must begin with an assessment of how the plan or policy meets the requirements of Agenda 21, and no plans or policies are allowed to contradict any part of the Agenda. Local authorities are audited by UN inspectors and the results of the audits are placed on the UN website. You can see how many local authorities in your country were bound by Agenda 21 in 2001 here. The number has increased significantly since then.

The official opening ceremony was conducted by the Dalai Lama and centered around a Viking long-ship that was constructed to celebrate the summit and sailed to Rio from Norway. The ship was appropriately named Gaia. A huge mural of a beautiful woman holding the earth within her hands adorned the entrance to the summit. Al Gore led the US delegation where he was joined by 110 Heads of State, and representatives of more than 800 NGO's.

Maurice Strong, Club of Rome member, devout Bahai, founder and first Secretary General of UNEP, has been the driving force behind the birth and imposition of Agenda 21. While he chaired the Earth Summit, outside his wife Hanne and 300 followers called the Wisdom-Keepers, continuously beat drums, chanted prayers to Gaia, and trended scared flames in order to "establish and hold the energy field" for the duration of the summit. You can view actual footage of these ceremonies on YouTube. During the opening speech Maurie Strong made the following statements:

"Current lifestyles and consumption patterns of the affluent middle class - involving high meat intake, use of fossil fuels, appliances, air-conditioning, and suburban housing - are not sustainable. A shift is necessary which will require a vast strengthening of the multilateral system, including the United Nations."

Among other things, the agenda called for a Global Biodiversity Assessment of the State of the Earth. Prepared by the UN Environmental Program (UNEP), this 1140 page document armed UN leaders with the "ecological basis, and moral authority" they needed to validate their global management system. The GBA concludes on page 863 that "the root causes of the loss of biodiversity are embedded in the way societies use resources. This world view is characteristic of large scale societies, heavily dependent on resources brought from considerable distances. It is a world view that is characterized by the denial of sacred attributes in nature, a characteristic that became firmly established about 2000 years ago with the Judeo-Christian-Islamic religious traditions. Eastern cultures with religious traditions such as Buddhism, Jainism and Hinduism did not depart as drastically from the perspective of humans as members of a community of beings including other living and non-living elements." In other words Christians and Moslems are to blame for the sorry state of the world because their religions do not involve worshipping "sacred nature."

So what exactly does Agenda 21 contain? It consists of 115 different and very specific programs designed to facilitate, or to force, the transition to Sustainable Development. The objective, clearly enunciated by the leaders of the Earth Summit, is to bring about a change in the present system of independent nations.

The agenda is broken up into 8 'program areas for action':

>> Agriculture

>> Biodiversity and Ecosystem Management

>> Education

>> Energy and Housing

>> Population

>> Public Health

>> Resources and recycling

>>Transportation,Sustainable Economic Development

Humanity stands at a defining moment in history. We are confronted with a perpetuation of disparities between and within nations, a worsening of poverty, hunger, ill health and illiteracy, and the continuing deterioration of the ecosystems on which we depend for our well-being. However, integration of environment and development concerns and greater attention to them will lead to the fulfillment of basic needs, improved living standards for all, better protected and managed ecosystems and a safer, more prosperous future. No nation can achieve this on its own, but together we can in a global partnership for sustainable development.

Considering its policies are woven into all the General Plans of the cities and counties, it's important for people to know where these policies are coming from. While many people support the United Nations for its 'peacemaking' efforts, hardly anyone knows that they have very specific land use policies that they would like to see implemented in every city, county, state and nation. The specific plan is called United Nations Agenda 21 Sustainable Development, which has its basis in Communitarianism.

By now, most Americans have heard of sustainable development but are largely unaware of Agenda 21.U.N.

Agenda 21 cites the affluence of Americans as being a major problem which needs to be corrected. It calls for lowering the standard of living for Americans so that the people in poorer countries will have more, a redistribution of wealth.

Although people around the world aspire to achieve the levels of prosperity we have in our country, and will risk their lives to get here, Americans are cast in a very negative light and need to be taken down to a condition closer to average in the world. Only then, they say, will there be social justice which is a cornerstone of the U.N. Agenda 21 plan.

Agenda 21 policies date back to the 70's but it got its real start in 1992 at the Earth Summit in Rio de Janeiro when President Bush signed onto it. *President Clinton took office the following year and created the President's Council on Sustainable Development to implement it in the United States. Made up of federal agencies, corporations, and non-profit groups, the President's Council on Sustainable Development moved quickly to ensure that all federal agencies would change their policies to comply with UN Agenda 21.*

A non-governmental organization called the International Council of Local Environmental Initiatives, ICLEI, is tasked with carrying out the goals of Agenda 21 worldwide. Remember: UN Agenda 21/Sustainable Development is a global plan that is implemented locally. Over 600 cities in the U.S. are members; our town joined in 2007. The costs are paid by taxpayers.

No matter where you live, I'll bet that there have been hundreds of condos built in the center of your town recently. Over the last ten years there has been a 'planning revolution' across the US. Your commercial, industrial, and multi-residential land was rezoned to 'mixed use.' Nearly everything that got approvals for development was designed the same way: ground floor retail with two stories of residential above with mixed use. Very hard to finance for construction, and very hard to manage since it has to have a high density of people in order to justify the retail. A lot of it is empty and most of the ground floor retail is empty too.

So what? Most of your towns provided funding and/or infrastructure development for these private projects. They used Redevelopment Agency funds. Your money. Specifically, your property taxes. Notice how there's very little money in your General Funds now, and most of that is going to pay police and fire? Your street lights are off, your parks are shaggy, your roads are pot-holed, and your hospitals are closing. The money that should be used for these things is diverted into the Redevelopment Agency. It's the only agency in government that can float a bond without a vote of the people. And they did that, and now you're paying off those bonds for the next 45 years with your property taxes. Did you know that? .

So, what does this have to do with Agenda 21?

Redevelopment is a tool used to further the Agenda 21 vision of remaking America's cities. With redevelopment, cities have the right to take property by eminent domain---against the will of the property owner, and give it or sell it to a private developer. By declaring an area of town 'blighted' (and in some cities over 90% of the city area has been declared blighted) the property taxes in that area can be diverted away from the General Fund. This constriction of available funds is impoverishing the cities, forcing them to offer less and less services, and reducing your standard of living. They'll be telling you that it's better, however, since they've put in nice street lights and colored paving. The money gets redirected into the Redevelopment Agency and handed out to favored developers building low income housing and mixed use. Smart Growth.

Cities have had thousands of condos built in the redevelopment areas and are telling you that you are terrible for wanting your own yard, for wanting privacy, for not wanting to be dictated to by a Condo Homeowner's Association Board, for being anti-social, for not going along to get along, for not moving into a cramped apartment downtown where they can use your property taxes for paying off that huge bond debt. But it's not working, and you don't want to move in there. So they have to make you.

Human habitation, as it is referred to now, is restricted to lands within the Urban Growth Boundaries of the city. Only certain building designs are permitted. Rural property is more and more restricted in what uses can be on it. Although counties say that they support agricultural uses, eating locally produced food, farmer's markets, etc., in fact there are so many regulations restricting water and land use (there are scenic corridors, inland rural corridors, baylands corridors, area plans, specific plans, redevelopment plans, huge fees, fines) that farmers are losing their lands altogether. County roads are not being paved.

The push is for people to get off of the land, become more dependent, and come into the cities. To get out of the suburbs and into the cities. Out of their private homes and into condos. Out of their private cars and onto their bikes.

Bikes. What does that have to do with it? I like to ride my bike and so do you. So what? Bicycle advocacy groups are very powerful now. Advocacy. A fancy word for lobbying, influencing, and maybe strong-arming the public and politicians. What's the connection with bike groups? National groups such as

Complete Streets, Thunderhead Alliance, and others, have training programs teaching their members how to pressure for redevelopment, and training candidates for office. It's not just about bike lanes; it's about remaking cities and rural areas to the 'sustainable model'. High density urban development without parking for cars is the goal. This means that whole towns need to be demolished and rebuilt in the image of sustainable development. Bike groups are being used as the 'shock troops' for this plan.

What plan? We're losing our homes since this recession/depression began, and many of us could never afford those homes to begin with. We got cheap money, used whatever we had to squeak into those homes, and now some of us lost them. We were lured, indebted, and sunk. Whole neighborhoods are empty in some places. Some are being bulldozed. Cities cannot afford to extend services outside of their core areas. Slowly, people will not be able to afford single family homes. Will not be able to afford private cars. Will be more dependent. More restricted. More easily watched and monitored.

This plan is a whole life plan. It involves the educational system, the energy market, the transportation system, the governmental system, the health care system, food production, and more.

The plan is to restrict your choices, limit your funds, narrow your freedoms, and take away your voice.

One of the ways is by using the Delphi Technique to 'manufacture consensus.' Another is to infiltrate community groups or actually start neighborhood associations with hand-picked 'leaders'. Another is to groom and train future candidates for local offices. Another is to sponsor non-governmental groups that go into schools and train children. Another is to offer federal and private grants and funding for city programs that further the agenda. Another is to educate a new generation of land use planners to require New Urbanism. Another is to convert factories to other uses, introduce energy measures that penalize manufacturing, and set energy consumption goals to pre-1985 levels. Another is to allow unregulated immigration in order to lower standards of living and drain local resources. (This is what Obama has been allowing)

What is Sustainable Development? According to its authors, the objective of sustainable development is to integrate economic, social and environmental policies in order to achieve reduced consumption, social equity, and the preservation and restoration of biodiversity. Sustainablists insist that every societal decision be based on environmental impact, focusing on three components; global land use, global education, and global population control and reduction.

Social Equity (Social injustice): Social justice is described as the right and opportunity of all people "to benefit equally from the resources afforded us by society and the environment." Redistribution of wealth. Private property is a social injustice since not everyone can build wealth from it. National sovereignty is a social injustice. Universal health care is a social injustice. All part of Agenda 21 policy.

Economic Prosperity: Public Private Partnerships (PPP). Special dealings between government and certain, chosen corporations which get tax breaks, grants and the government's power of Eminent Domain to implement sustainable policy. Government-sanctioned monopolies.

Local Sustainable Development policies: Smart Growth, Wildlands Project, Resilient Cities, Regional Visioning Projects, STAR Sustainable Communities, Green jobs, Green Building Codes, "Going Green," Alternative Energy, Local Visioning, facilitators, regional planning, historic preservation, conservation easements, development rights, sustainable farming, comprehensive planning, growth management, consensus.

Who is behind it? ICLEI – Local Governments for Sustainability (formally, International Council for Local Environmental Initiatives). Communities pay ICLEI dues to provide "local" community plans, software, training, etc. Addition groups include American Planning Council, The Renaissance Planning Group, International City/ County Management Group, aided by US Mayors Conference, National Governors Association, National League of Cities, National Association of County Administrators and many more private organizations and official government agencies. Foundation and government grants drive the process.

Where did it originate? The term Sustainable Development was first introduced to the world in the pages a 1987 report (Our Common Future) produced by the United Nations World Commission on Environmental and Development, authored by Gro Harlem Brundtland, VP of the World Socialist Party. The term was first offered as official UN policy in 1992, in a document called UN Sustainable Development Agenda 21, issued at the UN's Earth Summit, today referred to simply as Agenda 21.

What gives Agenda 21 Ruling Authority? More than 178 nations adopted Agenda 21 as official policy during a signing ceremony at the Earth Summit. US president George H.W. Bush signed the document for the US. In signing, each nation pledge to adopt the goals of Agenda 21. In 1995, President Bill Clinton, in compliance with Agenda 21, signed Executive Order #12858 to create the President's Council on Sustainable Development in order to "harmonize" US environmental policy with UN directives as outlined in Agenda 21. The EO directed all agencies of the Federal Government to work with state and local community governments in a joint effort "reinvent" government using the guidelines outlined in Agenda 21. As a result, with the assistance of groups like ICLEI, Sustainable Development is now emerging as government policy in every town, county and state in the nation.

Revealing Quotes From the Planners: "Agenda 21 proposes an array of actions which are intended to be implemented by EVERY person on Earth...it calls for specific changes in the activities of ALL people... Effective execution of Agenda 21 will REQUIRE a profound reorientation of ALL humans, unlike anything the world has ever experienced… " Agenda 21: The Earth Summit Strategy to Save Our Planet (Earthpress, 1993). Emphases – DR

"The realities of life on our planet dictate that continued economic development as we know it cannot be sustained…Sustainable development, therefore is a program of action for local and global economic reform – a program that has yet to be fully defined." The Local Agenda 21 Planning Guide, published by ICLEI, 1996.

"No one fully understands how or even, if, sustainable development can be achieved; however, there is growing consensus that it must be accomplished at the local level if it is ever to be achieved on a global basis." The Local Agenda 21 Planning Guide, published by ICLEI, 1996.

Agenda 21 and Private Property: "Land…cannot be treated as an ordinary asset, controlled by individuals and subject to the pressures and inefficiencies of the market. Private land ownership is also a principal instrument of accumulation and concentration of wealth, therefore contributes to social injustice." From the report from the 1976 UN's Habitat I Conference.

"Private land use decisions are often driven by strong economic incentives that result in several ecological and aesthetic consequences…The key to overcoming it is through public policy…" Report from the President's Council on Sustainable Development, page 112.

"**Current lifestyles and consumption patterns of the affluent middle class** – involving high meat intake, use of fossil fuels, appliances, home and work air conditioning, and suburban housing are not sustainable." Maurice Strong, Secretary General of the UN's Earth Summit, 1992.

Reinvention of Government: "We need a new collaborative decision process that leads to better decisions, more rapid change, and more sensible use of human, natural and financial resources in achieving our goals." Report from the President's Council on Sustainable Development.

"Individual rights will have to take a back seat to the collective." Harvey Ruvin, Vice Chairman, ICLEI. The Wildlands Project.

"We must make this place an insecure and inhospitable place for Capitalists and their projects – we must reclaim the roads and plowed lands, halt dam construction, tear down existing dams, free shackled rivers and return to wilderness millions of tens of millions of acres or presently settled land." Dave Foreman, Earth First.

What is not sustainable?

Ski runs, grazing of livestock, plowing of soil, building fences, industry, single family homes, paves and tarred roads, logging activities, dams and reservoirs, power line construction, and economic systems that fail to set proper value on the environment." UN's Biodiversity Assessment Report.

Hide Agenda 21's UN roots from the people:

"Participating in a UN advocated planning process would very likely bring out many of the conspiracy-fixated groups and individuals in our society... This segment of our society who fear 'one-world government' and a UN invasion of the United States through which our individual freedom would be stripped away would actively work to defeat any elected official who joined 'the conspiracy' by undertaking LA21. So we call our process something else, such as comprehensive planning, growth management or smart growth." J. Gary Lawrence, advisor to President Clinton's Council on Sustainable Development.

Smart Growth:

Smart growth is an urban planning and transportation theory that concentrates growth in compact walkable urban centers to avoid sprawl. It also advocates compact, transit-oriented, walkable, bicycle-friendly land use, including neighborhood schools, complete streets, and mixed-use development with a range of housing choices. The term 'smart growth' is particularly used in North America. In Europe and particularly the UK, the terms 'Compact City' or 'urban intensification' have often been used to describe similar concepts, which have influenced government planning policies in the UK, the Netherlands and several other European countries.

Smart growth values long-range, regional considerations of sustainability over a short-term focus. Its goals are to achieve a unique sense of community and place; expand the range of transportation, employment, and housing choices; equitably distribute the costs and benefits of development; preserve and enhance natural and cultural resources; and promote public health.

The concept of "smart growth" emerged in 1992 from the United Nation's adoption of Agenda 21 at the UN Conference on Environment and Development (UNCED) held in Rio de Janeiro, Brazil. Driven by "new guard" urban planners, architects, developers, community activists, and historic preservationists, it accepts that growth and development will continue to occur, and so seeks to direct that growth in an intentional, comprehensive way. smart growth principles are directed at developing sustainable communities that are good places to live, to do business, to work, and to raise families. Some of the fundamental aims for the benefits of residents and the communities are increasing family income and wealth, improving access to quality education, fostering livable, safe and healthy places, stimulating economic activity (both locally and regionally), and developing, preserving and investing in physical resources. There is a need to distinguish between smart growth "principles" and smart growth "regulations". The former are concepts and the latter their implementation, that is, how federal, state, and municipal governments choose to fulfill smart growth principles. One of the earliest efforts to establish smart growth forward as a regulatory framework were put forth by the American Planning Association. In 1997, the APA introduced a project called Growing Smart and published "Growing Smart Legislative Guidebook: Model Statutes for Planning and the Management of Change." The U.S. Environmental Protection Agency defines smart growth as "development that serves the economy, the community, and the environment. It changes the terms of the development debate away from the traditional growth/no growth question to how and where should new development be accommodated"

The Atlanta Beltline:

The Atlanta BeltLine is the most comprehensive revitalization effort ever undertaken in the City of Atlanta and among the largest, most wide-ranging urban redevelopment and mobility projects currently underway in the United States. This sustainable project is providing a network of public parks, multi-use trails and transit by re-using 22-miles of historic railroad corridors circling downtown and connecting 45 neighborhoods directly to each other The Atlanta BeltLine is transforming the city with a combination of rail, trail, greenspace, housing and art. It will ultimately connect 45 in town neighborhoods, provide first and last mile connectivity for regional transportation initiatives, and put Atlanta on a path to 21st century economic growth and sustainability. The beauty of the Atlanta BeltLine is that it offers not only modern conveyances and exciting new development, but it is a living, breathing part of our community; not simply a means of getting somewhere, but a destination unto itself. It offers a chance for Atlanta to redefine what it is to be a neighbor, to be a community, to be a region, and to share all that it has to offer

First conceived as a 1999 master's thesis by Georgia Tech student Ryan Gravel, the Atlanta BeltLine evolved from an idea, to a grassroots campaign of local citizens and civic leaders, into a robust new vision of an Atlanta dedicated to an integrated approach to transportation, land use, greenspace, and sustainable growth. The Atlanta BeltLine utilizes an existing 22-mile historic rail corridor that encircles the City of Atlanta as its foundation. Pedestrian friendly rail transit and 33 miles of multi-use trails will follow this corridor and spur off from it. The completion of the Atlanta BeltLine will bring together 45 in town neighborhoods and also link them to the entire metropolitan Atlanta region through a collection of transit offerings.

Very soon it will be mandatory for us all to move out of the suburbs and country and live in these villages.

143

10

GET YOUR CHILDREN OUT OF THE PUBLIC SCHOOL SYSTEM

Satan's plan is to indoctrinate and program the world to accept the Antichrist and his Luciferic doctrine via the media and our school system. These occult theses and teachings are everywhere in our society today thru entertainment, movies, television shows, music and music videos, books and cartoon shows for children.

This insures the Luciferic Doctrine will not seem "alien" to the word when Antichrist comes as the world has slowly been taught this all along.

Major movies such as Star Wars and Harry Potter have done much to promote their religion of light and love and magic. By the time the average child in America is 16 years old, they have been exposed to over 1000 hours of Luciferic Programming.

Obama's agenda now is focused upon taking over our school system to be able to indoctrinate our children, brain wash them , control them and teach them to become dependent upon the government.

First he has put into office over the Education System ungodly homosexual, perverted people.

He is known to the United States as the "Safe Schools Czar:" a special advisor in the White House responsible for helping formulate policies designed to keep US public schools "safe and drug free." But US pro-family leaders know Kevin Jennings as something more: a highly influential homosexual activist, who admitted in a book on his childhood that a deep-seated hatred of God and religious believers began when he fully embraced a homosexual lifestyle and bid God farewell with the words, "Screw you, buddy."

Jennings's official position within the Obama Administration is the Assistant Deputy Secretary, who directs the Office of Safe and Drug Free Schools under US Department of Education Secretary Arne Duncan.

Duncan is a veteran of Chicago's public school system, who proposed and approved controversial plans for a special public high school designed for homosexuals.

Jennings brings to the Education Department his experience as the cofounder and executive director of the Gay, Lesbian, and Straight Education Network (GLSEN), where in keeping with that organization's mission; he concentrated his energies on developing and advocating classroom curricula for public schools that would re-educate school-children to embrace homosexuality. As a key part of their strategy to advance their agenda and change the culture, GLSEN leaders say they specifically target children as young as kindergarten in order to begin a "saturation process," that forms the imagination with positive impressions of the homosexual lifestyle, and so pre-cognitively influences the way a child perceives the world and makes judgments on right and wrong.

Bill Donohue, a civil rights leader and President of the Catholic League, stated that Kevin Jennings "has a history of bashing Christians" which appears deeply rooted in his decision at 17 years-old that he was a homosexual and God was to blame for his feelings of guilt and shame.

Donohue draws the conclusion from Jennings's own book called "Mama's Boy, Preacher's Son: A Memoir," published in 2006 by Beacon Press, which deals with his upbringing by his father, the Baptist minister, and his mother, the non-believer and anti-Catholic. Jennings writes that he came to this "new attitude toward God" following a masturbatory experience that was prompted by fantasies of two "hot guys" taking off their shirts in his home.

"Before, I was the one who was failing God; now I decided He was the one who had failed me," wrote Jennings. "I decided I had done nothing wrong: He had, by promising to 'set you free' and never delivering on His promise. What had He done for me, other than make me feel shame and guilt? Squat. Screw you, buddy - I don't need you around anymore, I decided."

Jennings concludes by saying that for years afterwards he "reacted violently to anyone who professed any kind of religion" and it would be decades later before he opened a Bible again.

But Jennings still retains contempt for observant believers on what he calls "the religious right."

In fact, Jennings told a gathering of fellow activists in 2000 that conservative-minded Christians were "hard-core bigots" who should "drop dead."

But the GLSEN founder had the group laughing by telling them he really wanted to just say to them: "f*** you!"

Jennings was also on the board of advisers for a 2001 PBS documentary-style film that slammed the Boy Scouts of America for their policy of excluding homosexuals from their membership and was promoted at "gay pride" festivals to mobilize homosexuals against the Scouts.

Further concern has arisen about Jennings concerning his history as a former drug abuser, and as a school counselor back in 1988, who failed to report a sexually active homosexual relationship between an adult and a boy, then a sophomore high school student. Instead Jennings counseled the boy named "Brewster" on maintaining the relationship with the adult, which began in a bus stop bathroom.

During his tenure as GLSEN's executive director, Jennings also promoted homosexual conferences that featured GLSEN presenters hosting extremely graphic and detailed workshops to teenagers about all the mechanics and variations of homosexual intercourse.

Obama's new school curriculum is called "Common Core". Obama Pushes Common Core Standards Including Incest & Explicit Sex.

Have you heard about the Common Core? These are educational standards that have been adopted by 45 states over the past few years which are now being implemented this year. Of course, these standards are actually an Obama Regime invention; basically they came with a bribe for the states that have adopted them: in order for the states to be able to compete for $4.35 billion in Race to the Top federal funds, they had to adopt these standards. Or, as the administration phrased it, they needed to adopt "college and career ready standards," which is basically what the common core claims to be.

But let's take a closer look into some of what these "common core" standards really mean in practical terms. On the reading front, 11th graders will be using a book titled "The Bluest Eye, by Toni Morrison. Unfortunately, most parents would find this book to be morally offensive and probably not let their child real it if given a choice.

Some of the topics included in this book are pedophilia, incest, rape, and (of course) just plain old sex.

Making matters even worse, this is an Oprah recommended book about a young black girl who wishes she were white. The fact that Oprah has recommended this, after her recent crazy antics, should be enough to turn off most people right there. But this book is surprisingly graphic and detailed in its accounts of many of the topics discussed above. Additionally, even a quick review of this book shows that is not meant to teach the kids about either the beauty of the English language or how to write well. In fact, the language and grammar is surprisingly bad for a supposedly professional writer like Morrison.

Of course, the common core reading overview description that is presented on their website and even given out to parents who request a copy does not detail these facts. In fact their 'representative excerpt is actually quite benign. The idiots don't even have the guts to actually put out there what they are really trying to do!

While I am going to spare the gory details of actually reprinting the smut itself, suffice it to say that these passages would make a good pornographer blush and laugh. Blush, because they are quite graphic and laugh because they could likely write better than Ms. Morrison! And get this, Morrison herself even gave an interview about this book giving her motives behind it (be ready to have shock). Basically, she wanted to be very graphic as well as, get this, non-judgmental! This includes her passages regarding incest and pedophilia! She even goes so far as to say that she wants the reader to feel like they are "co-conspirator" with the rapist...and that she took great pains to avoid portraying them as wrong in order to show that everyone has their own problems.

Oh, yes, she also describes the rape, incest, and pedophilia as "friendly," "innocent," and even "tender."

Wow. Before I forget, this book is in the top 10 list of most contested books in the country.

Common Core is Obamas way of dummying down the American children so he can infiltrate them with his doctrines and agendas.

Another thing is that if we look even closer at the common core as a whole, it is not having an overall improvement on education. In New York State, which was one of the first states to adopt these standards, they have caused test scores to plummet, with only 31 percent passing. Plus, the failure rates were highest among the neediest students: only 3.2 percent of English language learners passed, and only 17 percent of black students passed.

So, Mr. Obama, what are we doing with these common core standards? Just throwing money at the problem without taking time to really improve anything or even understand what is needed? Or is it just designed to throw smut at our students and hope they shut up and play nice in the corner.

Elementary school children are being taught that the government is their family.

Fourth-grade students in Illinois are learning that "government is like a nation's family" because it sets rules and takes care of needs such as health care and education.

So says a worksheet for social studies homework that was distributed to students at East Prairie School in Skokie, Ill, complete with a drawing of Uncle Sam cradling a baby that represents the citizens.

Students are then prompted to answer 10 questions comparing government and families, including how their family provides for their health care needs and how the government does the same, and what rules families set and what rules government sets.

The worksheet it titled, "What is Government?" and then goes on to answer that question.

"Government is all of the agencies, departments, organizations, groups, individuals in a nation who make, carry out, enforce, and manage conflicts about rules and laws," the worksheet says.

"Government is like a nation's family." Families take care of children and make sure they are safe, healthy and educated, and free to enjoy life. Families encourage children to be independent hardworking and responsible, it continues. Families make and enforce rules and give appropriate punishments when rules are broken. Government does these things for its citizens, too.

The worksheet asks the following questions:

1. How does your family keep you safe?

2. How does the government keep its citizens safe?

3. How does your family keep you healthy?

4. How does the government keep its citizens healthy?

5. How does your family help you learn and become educated?

6. How does the government help its citizens learn and become educated?

7. What kind of rules does your family have for you?

8. What kind of rules does government have for its citizens?

9. How does your family punish you when you break the rules?

10. How does government punish citizens who break the law?

The government's aim is to get rid of all schools and curriculum and replace it with theirs- The Common Core. Obama coerced the states into his program buy offering them money. After they accepted the money and the program they are seeing that this program is Anti-American and many are trying to give the money back and stop the program.

The government's goal is to brainwash our children with their propaganda and ways of thinking. That is why they have come up with the "Common Core" school curriculum that is mandatory.

Obama has sanctioned the new global educational reform called "Common Core," a United Nations-friendly curriculum that will end freedom and success in America. The curriculum is based on the "humans cause climate change" lie that Al Gore and his ilk are perpetually peddling. If you disagree with this theory you are likened to a racist (which is their go-to rally cry). Did you hear, just this week, Al Gore was caught in another lie about climate change?!

Obama forced states to sign on to Common Core by dangling money in front of them at the worst possible economic moment, bribing them to sign on to his "Race to the Top" program and essentially nationalizing American education into his one world order, Agenda 21-influenced worldview.

Common Core is a socialism change agent that is beginning now, and it will hook the youngest members of our communities—our children—into the net of police state government.

It is not voluntary, and there is no way to opt-out.

You and your kids don't have a choice. Obama has decided what curriculum is right for you, and it is beginning now. We must get rid of Common Core before our kids turn into a nation of sheep.

Parents and teachers are being completely removed from the education process and the government is stepping in to take over.

The Common Core program is being marketed by the administration as an innovative, wonderful educational curriculum that will advance the hearts and minds of American kids and put them in a position to be competitive with the rest of the education world.

Do not be fooled; it is anything but competitive. We have peered behind the curtain and you need to be aware of what we found. Start connecting the dots with us:

Make no mistake, this is about redistribution. The Common Core program is all about control of another aspect of our economy and about indoctrinating our kids into believing that his agenda of socialism, equality and environmental justice. Our kids will not learn about

155

the most moral financial system in the world, capitalism and free markets. No, they will learn that capitalists are ruining the planet and our atmosphere while destroying the world!

Kids are the first stop on the bus to changing America via Agenda 21. This is why the Common Core program is so intrusive and so skewed against American ideals. The Left needs to get 'em young and get 'em hooked on the idea of a government that takes care of every aspect of the lives and throughout adulthood.

Common Core lowers the academic standards for American kids and creates an "if it feels good, it's okay" mentality.

A Stanford professor says that Common Core will put American kids at least two years behind high-achieving countries in math. Kentucky did a Common Core pilot program and saw proficiency rates drop by 30 percent. This is probably because math doesn't mean figuring out numbers and equations anymore and there are no longer really any wrong answers. It's all about how you think and feel about a problem. A Common Core video explains to teachers if a child comes to the conclusion that 3x4=11, it's not necessarily wrong, as long as that child can show you how they came up with that number and if the way makes any sense, the result is just not that important.

The United Nations Educational, Scientific and Cultural Organization have no business butting into the American education system. But, they are. Liberals want

U.N. bureaucrats to build a curriculum for America that gets kids to welcome the state as adoptive parents.

They need them to buy into an Agenda 21 sustainability mindset that teaches them that humans are harming the planet, Western civilization is bad, and one global, socialist society needs to rule the land in order to maintain peace and justice.

Common Core spends 8 weeks on the United Nations Declaration of Human Rights (teaching many classes through Scientology videos) that everyone has a right to social security, a job, housing and to join a union), and much less time on the U.S. Constitution and Bill of Rights.

The curriculum demonizes capitalism and free markets (what's left of it) of the United States by using math problems to tell our children that being rich is unfair and the rich are taking from the poor. We saw some of this hatred come out in 2012 when the Teacher's Union released the video showing the rich urinating on the poor located below them!

And what is really alarming is that parents, educators, and legislators do not know they are getting our children into a deal with the devil! It takes away rights of states in control their own schools and districts. We are actually hearing that parents are not allowed to enter some schools, are not given their child's textbooks as they are stored in class, and will not have a local school board to meet with and discus local issues and concerns.

President Obama and his radical friends are deconstructing our history and our culture by taking away the classics that teach right from wrong, individual responsibility and citizenship. No, our children are "Citizens of the World" and by now I hope you are connecting the dots on Communism, Socialism, and Marxism!

A history textbook already in classrooms for several years spends pages upon pages on Islam without one chapter on Christianity or Judaism. Any mentions of Christianity's past reference "massacres", while Islamic history teaches of "takeovers" and speaks of how welcoming members of society were to Islam. The book states that Jesus "proclaimed" himself the Messiah, and Mohammed "was the prophet". No "proclamation" there.

Your kids will be reading far fewer classic novels and more "information" texts such as government documents and technical manuals. They will read computer manuals and EPA white papers instead of traditional literature. Maybe even Obama's "Dreams From My Father" will be required reading. U.S. education will now be controlled at the federal level. Parents, teachers and states will have no freedom to tailor lessons to their needs.

The curriculum will re-write history and teach that environmental concerns are the most important, and serving the state is an ultimate goal. But, beyond the lowered academic requirements, we are most concerned about the large database being gathered on our children.

Common Core requires extensive data to be kept on all children in a database called in Bloom. It will store your student's name, address, social security number, blood type, hair color, weight, test scores, nicknames, religion, attitudes, income level, medical history, psychological evaluations, bus stop times and political affiliation. Participation is mandatory, even for kids in private and home schools.

Let's look at why the state could possibly need so much information on our kids. One word: control. From Kindergarten through their twenties, the "state" will make assessments on what type of student your child is, and what kind of job they are best suited for. Barack Obama and his socialist backers are going to restructure the United States so that everyone is told what their ability is and they will be working at a menial government job making menial government money and thinking the federal government would pick up the slack for their insurance, their housing, and their retirement.

This data collection conveniently ties back to the "Affordable Healthcare Act," which authorizes forced federal visits to your home if the government deems you "high-risk." If Common Core data on your kids designates them as "high risk," the Health and Human Services' website says the government can come to your home if you fall under the following "risky" categories:

*Families where mom is not yet 21.

*Families where someone is a tobacco user.

*Families where children have low student achievement, developmental delays, or disabilities.

*Kids living with individuals who are serving or formerly served in the armed forces, including such families that have members of the armed forces who have had multiple deployments outside the United States.

Constitutional attorney and author Kent Masterson Brown states, "This is not a 'voluntary' program. The eligible entity receiving the grant for performing the home visits is to identify the individuals to be visited and intervene so as to meet the improvement benchmarks. A homeschooling family, for instance, may be subject to "intervention" in "school readiness" and "social-emotional developmental indicators." A farm family may be subject to "intervention" in order to "prevent child injuries." The sky is the limit.

The government can acquire information like this through Common Core, Obamacare data collection, the NSA database, the FBI database or one of the other 70 databases on the American people. This information is already being used to take away our civil liberty as highlighted in many cases around the country. In New York, law abiding citizens are getting letters from the State Police telling them to turn over their guns or else! Or else, the State Police (SWAT outfitted) will come to their house and get them! And HIPAA is not here to protect you my friends. No, instead, this president is using it to take away any semblance of privacy we might have left - our personal health records.

The main goal of the Privacy Rule is "...to assure that individuals' health information is properly protected while allowing the flow of health information needed to provide and promote high quality healthcare and to protect the public's health and well-being!! There it is the statement no one knew was in there because it wasn't written yet!

And, why in the world, is your family's political affiliation being collected as part of the Common Core database? Will your political beliefs be used against your child? Will you endure a forced federal visit because you disagree with the current party in power? This is Big Brother if we have ever seen it! Everything you say and do is being collected by the government and can and will be used against you. They have already targeted conservatives through the IRS...now they are now coming for your kids via Common Core!

Is this the future we want for our most precious resource—our children?

Parents and teachers are being completely removed from the education process and the government is stepping in to take over. Culturally, Common Core wants to mold our kids into dutiful little Leftists, using various bio-analysis tools.

The "curriculum" calls for: "Four parallel streams of affective sensors" will be employed to effectively "measure" each child. The "facial expression camera," for instance, "is a device that can be used to detect emotion.... Other devices, such as the "posture analysis seat," "pressure mouse," and "wireless skin conductance sensor," which looks like a wide, black bracelet strapped to a child's wrist, are all designed to collect "physiological response data from a biofeedback apparatus that measures blood volume, pulse, and galvanic skin response to examine student frustration."

Common Core seeks to change behavior. One of the agencies responsible for testing is the American Institute for Research, or AIR. They are one of the largest behavioral and social science research organizations in the world, and are focused on changing behavior. AIR distributes LGBT propaganda to schools and believes not only in the sexualization of children, but in labeling and counseling those children at a very young age.

The documents state in black and white what will be taught: "Students need opportunities to engage in cooperative and active learning strategies, and sufficient time must be allocated for students to practice skills relating to sexuality education."

This curriculum was developed behind closed doors and there are no meeting notes. Although they say it will be internationally benchmarked, there is no other country in the world that anyone can point to with a Common Core curriculum. But, working behind closed doors implementing, writing standards, are some of President Obama's former friends and associates from back-in-the-day. Like one of the scariest people in education, Linda Darling-Hammond. Ms. Hammond may look like a Libertarian, but don't let that fool you because she is one of the most radical, progressive educators you will ever meet. Hammond is a close associate and colleague of William, BILL AYERS, the former head of the terrorist group known as The Weather Underground. Bill is buddies with Obama, even threw Obama's first fundraiser.

So the new code-words for redistribution of wealth are "your zip code", as in "Your zip code should not determine your education. Your zip code should not define your job" or your whatever they want to fill-in-the-blank. The mission of Hammond's work on the Committee for Equity and Excellence in education was outlined in a report called, "A Strategy for Education Equity and Excellence." This report tells you how this so-called educational reform is nothing more than another deception to re-distribute the wealth through education.

"The time has come for bold action by the states— and the federal government—to redesign and reform the funding of our nation's public schools. Achieving equity and excellence requires sufficient resources that are distributed based on student need, not zip code, and that are efficiently used."

This report goes on to make some incredible statements about our constitution. "We have, however, learned from past efforts and believe we are in a position to move forward. There is no constitutional barrier to a greater federal role in financing K-12 education. It is, rather, a question of our nation's civic and political will; the modest federal contribution that today amounts to approximately 10 percent of national K-12 spending is a matter of custom, not a mandate.

The federal government must take bold action in specific areas."

Federal contribution means more taxes leaving your sate and less coming back!

Ohio school superintendent Mick Zais, "the standards were adopted hastily by a select few and are a one-size-fits-all solution that won't serve students well."

Providence College English Literature Professor Anthony Esolen, "What appalls me the most about the Common Core Standards is the cavalier contempt for great works of human art, thought and literary form...We are not programming machines; we are teaching children."

The Brookings Institution says, "The empirical evidence suggests that the Common Core will have little effect on American students' achievement."

A Heritage Foundation Issue Brief says, "Common Core's standards not only present a serious threat to state and local education authority, but also put academic quality at risk."

Common Core: Is Obama's mandatory school curriculum being forced upon all states. It is a Lesson Plan for Raising Up Compliant, Non Thinking Citizens; there are several methods for controlling a population. The government is going after our children to make them solders of the government.

The Curriculum dummies down our children and fills their minds with communist, socialist doctrines. It no longer even teaches them to write in cursive. You can watch a video on youtube that was shown to a middle school elementary class that teaches them to pledge their allegiance to Obama not to the country.

The government is indoctrinating them into compliance from an early age through the schools, discouraging them from thinking for themselves while rewarding them for regurgitating whatever the government, through its so-called educational standards, dictates they should be taught.

Those who founded America believed that an educated citizenry knowledgeable about their rights was the surest means of preserving freedom. If so, then the inverse should also hold true: that the surest way for a government to maintain its power and keep the citizenry in line is by rendering them ignorant of their rights and unable to think for themselves.

When viewed in light of the government's ongoing attempts to amass power at great cost to Americans—in terms of free speech rights, privacy, due process, etc.—the debate over Common Core State Standards, which would transform and nationalize school curriculum from kindergarten through 12th grade, becomes that much more critical.

Essentially, these standards, which were developed through a partnership between big government and corporations, in the absence of any real input from parents or educators with practical, hands-on classroom experience, and are being rolled out in 45 states and the District of Columbia, will create a generation of test-takers capable of little else, molded and shaped by the federal government and its corporate allies into what it considers to be ideal citizens.

A St. Tammany Parish School Board committee on Thursday overwhelmingly adopted a resolution calling on Gov. Bobby Jindal, state Education Superintendent John White and BESE to abandon the Common Core standards and testing.

The resolution adopted by the board's Human Resources and Education Committee goes to the full School Board next week. But because the committee is comprised of the full board, it's likely the resolution will be formally adopted and sent to Jindal, White, the Board of Elementary and Secondary Education and the 144 members of the state Legislature.

The resolution asks the state to remove "the St. Tammany Parish public school system and the other school districts in Louisiana" from the implementation of the Common Core standards and testing by the Partnership for Assessment of Readiness for College and Careers, known as PARCC.

Save for a few amendments by board members, the committee had little debate on the measure. A few of the 40 or so Common Core opponents gathered in the School Board's meeting room in Covington spoke, thanking committee members for the resolution.

"I feel that if we say this enough we might get it," parent Nancy Hendrick said, later adding, "Why would we trade a curriculum and standards that work so well?"

The committee's adoption of the resolution -- 13 of the board's 15 members attended the meeting -- comes after a series of public meetings during which board members got an earful from parents angered by the new standards.

The Common Core State Standards, and the state's implementation of them, have become a lightning rod for criticism from some parents and elected officials. Opponents have complained that the math being taught is confusing and overly complex, that children might have to read objectionable texts in language arts, that the companies running the testing are storing private student data, and that the new standards are essentially the federalizing of school curriculum.

Following are graphic and explicit excerpts from The Bluest Eye, which is on the Common Core's list of exemplar texts for 11th graders. If you are easily offended you may want to skip them and go straight to the story. (Note from editor: Even heavily edited, this is still very graphic.)

Pages 162-163: "A bolt of desire ran down his genitals...and softening the lips of his anus. . . . He wanted to f*** her—tenderly. But the tenderness would not hold. The tightness of her vagina was more than he could bear. His soul seemed to slip down his guts and fly out into her, and the gigantic thrust he made into her then provoked the only sound she made. Removing

167

himself from her was so painful to him he cut it short and snatched his genitals out of the dry harbor of her vagina. She appeared to have fainted."

Page 174: "He further limited his interests to little girls. They were usually manageable . . . His sexuality was anything but lewd; his patronage of little girls smacked of innocence and was associated in his mind with cleanliness." And later, this same pedophile notes, "I work only through the Lord. He sometimes uses me to help people."

Page 181: "The little girls are the only things I'll miss. Do you know that when I touched their sturdy little t*** and bit them—just a little—I felt I was being friendly?—If I'd been hurting them, would they have come back? . . . they'd eat ice cream with their legs open while I played with them. It was like a party."

Pages 84-85: "He must enter her surreptitiously, lifting the hem of her nightgown only to her navel. He must rest his weight on his elbows when they make love, to avoid hurting her breasts...When she senses some spasm about to grip him, she will make rapid movements with her hips, press her fingernails into his back, suck in her breath, and pretend she is having an orgasm. She might wonder again, for the six hundredth time, what it would be like to have that feeling while her husband's penis is inside her."

Pages 130-131: "Then he will lean his head down and bite my t** . . . I want him to put his hand between my legs, I want him to open them for me. . . I stretch my legs open, and he is on top of me...He would die rather than take his thing out of me. Of me. I take my fingers out of his and put my hands on his behind…"

Pages 148-149: "With a violence born of total helplessness, he pulled her dress up, lowered his trousers and underwear. 'I said get on wid it. An'make it good, n*****, Come on c***. Faster. You ain't doing nothing for her.' He almost wished he could do it— hard, long, and painfully, he hated her so much.

Book: Dreaming in Cuban by Cristina Garcia.: This is a 10th grade literature book that was used in my son's class at Buena High School in Sierra Vista, Arizona. The whole class read this book out loud during class. Everyone in the class had a copy of this book. This book was recommended by Common Core Curriculum.

The following excerpt is taken from page 80: "Hugo and Felicia stripped in their room, dissolving easily into one another, and made love against the whitewashed walls. Hugo bit Felicia's breast and left purplish bands of bruises on her upper thighs. He knelt before her in the tub and massaged black Spanish soap between her legs. He entered her repeatedly from behind. "Felicia learned what pleased him. She tied his arms above his head with their underclothing and slapping him sharply when he asked." 'You're my bitch,'" Hugo said, groaning. "In the morning he left, promising to return in the summer."

Yes, "Dreaming in Cuban" by Cristina Garcia is indeed recommended in the Common Core Standards for

English Language Arts & Literacy in History/Social Studies, Science, and Technical Subjects.

Because the Common Core Standards Initiative ties teachers' evaluations to the scores their students make on the Common Core assessments, teachers are pressured to teach the Common Core Text Exemplars and Sample Performance Tasks (Appendix B).

" By directing teachers and students to the interview with Cristina Garcia, it is easy to see that Common Core becomes basically a marketing tool to launch Cristina Garcia's latest book – King of Cuba – which undoubtedly has more pornographic, raunchy, inappropriate, lascivious, prurient, and sexualized language in it.

Common Core recommends that teachers teach many multicultural, politically correct books and gives teachers and students web links to authors' sites, thus influencing students to purchase more books by these same authors.

With Common Core demanding that teachers teach informational text from 50% to 70% of the time, the time-honored, character-building classics will be dropped because they take large blocks of time to teach. In their place, offensive, sexualized books such as Dreaming in Cuban will take over students' classrooms (and their minds).

Not only are such books highly offensive to those who hold traditional values (e.g., belief in personal responsibility, self- discipline, respect for authority, self-control, a solid work ethic, respect for other people, traditional marriage), but they also serve a purpose for those who are trying to indoctrinate this and future generations to hate America and to trash American exceptionalism. A steady diet of portraying ethnic/racial characters always as victims and saturating these books with gutter language is bound to warp students' minds.

11

THE GREAT PERSECUTION OF GOD'S PEOPLE

With the presidency of Obama our American Society has changed forever. He has been a pawn used to open up the doors to begin the Great Persecution of God's born again Church. He has passed laws and will continue to do so that will pave the way for our total destruction, and for the total liberation of the followers of the American Jesus.

The Holy Spirit is writing this book to warn you about the coming great persecution in America and the world and to prepare you for it.

Everything that we have known in America is about to change forever. This had to happen sometime to pave the way for the Anti-christ to rule the world and the Great Tribulation to come about. We have witnessed it with our own eyes, in our very own lifetime. This is truly the generation that the Jesus of the Bible will return in, but before he does the American Jesus must rule the world and promote the "Man of Sin" whom we call the Anti-christ and his ungodly agendas.

The laws have been passed now in America for the followers of the American Jesus to rise up and rule with their devilish agendas and programs. It is only a matter of time until they implement our total destruction.

The days of meeting together in public churches is coming to a close. The days of preaching Biblical principles from the pulpit are coming to a close.

We have been "targeted for destruction". Obama's laws now proclaim us as terrorists and haters and we will no longer be tolerated in America. The American people that are serving the American Jesus have their eyes blinded to God's truths and will begin to persecute us and hand us over to the authorities to be put into prison camps and exterminated.

We have nothing to look forward to in our future now but great persecution, imprisonment, and death. Those of us who have our spiritual eyes opened up will be led to prepare ourselves and our family's safety bunkers and store up food and commodities now so when these days come we will have a place of safety to hide out in.

First we will begin to experience great persecution on our jobs and many will lose them. We will begin to be unable to buy or sale anything without jeopardizing our Christian beliefs.

Our days of living in America the blessed are now over! There is not anything here for us any longer to look forward to as far as living the American dream is concerned. They will consider us the terrorists and the haters and our lives are about to change forever. Obama's laws have declared that we be arrested and put into prison camps because of our beliefs.

Obama is about to change America into a "police state". The government's armed guards are going to be present in our streets and at our doors to bring about the changes that are in the process in America.

The target is not the criminals, the rapists, the gang members, the homosexuals, the thief's or the murderers. The target is the "Christians". We are the number one target. It has already begun. The government is targeting the Christian businesses. Very soon we will not be able to own our own businesses.

Obama is being led and guided by Satan to turn America into a socialistic police state. He has passed laws that have taken away our freedom of speech and many other rights that we had under the Constitution. He is taking control of us. He is doing his own will. His agenda is to create a One World Government where Islam rules.

He has already passed so many laws that are detrimental to Christians that it would take too long for me to list them all. But let me give you an over view.

The passing of ObamaCare is the beginning of the Mark of the Beast. It is forcing the American people to do things the government's way. It does not matter if you believe that God will heal you and you don't want to buy medical insurance. You have too! You are being forced to! This is the first of many things we will have to be forced to do! The ObamaCare also has a stipulation that they can tract a medical device by implanting a device under the skin. The people of America have no idea that they are one step closer to the Mark of the Beast.

Obama will be in office for about three more years. During this time we will see many things happen that will be detrimental to Christians. He plans to control the American people. (He will probably change

America's laws and keep himself in office after his term expires).

He is tracing and monitoring the American people. Obama uses the mask of terrorist control to infringe upon our freedoms.

The U.S. National Security Agency is able to crack protective measures on iPhones, BlackBerry and Android devices, giving it access to users' data on all major smartphones, according to a report Sunday in German news weekly Der Spiegel.

The magazine cited internal documents from the NSA and its British counterpart GCHQ in which the agencies describe setting up dedicated teams for each type of phone as part of their effort to gather intelligence on potential threats such as terrorists.

The data obtained this way includes contacts, call lists, SMS traffic, notes and location information, Der Spiegel reported. The documents don't indicate that the NSA is conducting mass surveillance of phone users but rather that these techniques are used to eavesdrop on specific individuals, the magazine said.

It seems very clear to me, and there is a voluminous amount of evidence to support the conclusion that a government conspiracy is in fact already in place. Every move we make is monitored. Every call we make can be traced. Every email we send can be captured. Every financial transaction we do is data-based. We can't travel even in our own country without being strip-searched and abused by the cretins at TSA. And if the government decides for no reason at all to label us as "enemy combatants," they can throw us in prison and torture or kill us without even the benefit of trial. So why would anyone think that this government could not and would not take the next step in its progression of control? That next step is Martial Law, and once implemented might turn out to be the final step in ending our history of freedom!

When martial law officially comes to America, it will also come to Canada. The United States Northern Command (NORTHCOM) which has announced that it is ready to impose martial law is a tool of a larger political project to bring America, Canada and Mexico under a dictatorial political, financial, legal and military union that will compete with the fascistic European Union.

Through Obamas terrorist control he will target us Christians and it's only a matter of time until he begins to arrest us.

Christian businesses are already being shut down because of trying to uphold Christian values. The law now says that business owners cannot deny public accommodations based on sexual orientation or gender identity.

Aaron and Melissa Klein were forced to close their bakery, "Sweet Cakes by Melissa", after refusing to make a wedding cake for a lesbian couple.

Marking what is likely the end of a legal battle that has lasted for the past seven years, the New Mexico Supreme Court has ruled that an Albuquerque wedding photographer can be held liable under the state's anti-discrimination laws for refusing to provide service to a same-sex couple saying the First Amendment does not permit businesses that offer services for a profit to choose whom to serve.

Wake up Pastors! The days of meeting together in Churches is about over! Obama is coming after you! He will begin to press the law that states you cannot discriminate against marring same sex couples. You will be forced to marry lesbians or you will be shut down by the government!

Christians are being run out of businesses right now! And the Christian churches in America will be targeted next. Many of our Pastors will succumb to this evil and marry same sex couples because they don't want to lose their livelihood. Others will begin to meet underground.

We are entering into the days of the early Christian Church. We are entering into being persecuted for our faith. Many will be arrested and put into prison. Many will be killed.

Soon, something major is going to happen in America. It will be called a huge terrorists attack. (It will really be instigated by the government) Then Marshall Law will be implemented. Christians will be the targets. We will be rounded up and tortured for our faith.

It will be a replay of the early Church days when Nero the Roman Emperor set the city on fire and blamed it on the Christians so he could kill them. The Church is going to go out the same way they came in which is in the midst of great persecution.

And The Beast will wage war with the saints for forty and two months and He shall overcome them". (Rev.13:7)

"And all who will not worship The Beast shall be killed." "And I saw the souls of those beheaded for the witness of Jesus who would not worship the beast and receive his mark on their right hand and forehead.(Rev.20:4) And I saw a great multitude, greater than any man could number come out of the Great tribulation, having washed their robes in The Blood of The Lamb."(Rev.7:14)

Antichrist will teach "Peace thru Unity" and that the Christian religion and its followers bring division and "bad karma". So when all Christians are killed and all Bibles burned peace and love and harmony shall fill the earth.

The Illuminati plans to use Obama to trigger WWIII. This will be a war that will kill over 100 million people and guarantee the crash of all world economies and the establishment of their new world order (666) of Lucifer.

On May 19, 2011 Obama turned against Israel along with the EU, Russia, China, Britain, the Muslim world and now the Vatican. By Obama calling for a Palestinian state with "1967 borders" (that would spell the destruction of Israel).

The Obama agenda against Israel insures the Illuminati that WWIII will be triggered, as Israel will be forced to attack Iran to stop their nuclear threat. Obama was told to allow Iran to continue their nuclear weapons program and he did. This will trigger the Apocalypse.

In 1928 when America was faced with a National recession, democrats dramatically raised taxes and restricted trade. The result was the crash of the USA stock market and the Great Depression. The Obama white house is repeating history and this will trigger the worst economic depression in the history of planet earth. This will start with the collapse of small businesses and mass unemployment.

The next great depression is about to happen. The Obama Economic Plan will crash the USA stock market and our dollar. Banks, corporations and farms will be under government control as Martial Law is declared, supported by United Nations Forces. America will be a land filled with tent cities, ghost towns and bread lines, Churches converted to homeless shelters and "Sex for Food" the accepted means of survival. Armed Gangs will roam the streets like animals and possibly one third of America will be dead from Swine Flu or some form of pestilence that the government turns upon the people. Obama just as with communist Russia, China and Nazi Germany seeks to disarm the American people as quickly as possible.

Then, in this downtrodden, broken and poverty stricken state, America will be ready to accept any plan that gives them food and shelter and this is the plan of the Anti-christ, for a one world government, based upon 666, Upon Lucifer (Satan) as God.

The war that Obama will trigger against Israel is the final nail in the coffin of the world economies.

Just as the early Church was hunted down and rounded up and fed to the lions as the spectators cheered on, so will the government and ungodly people begin to do the Christians in America. We will be called the "Haters" and the "Terrorists" and the government will have a zero tolerance for us.

The Pentagon has labeled Born Again Christians as terrorists:

The Pentagon is the nation's hub for military activity. One would think this nerve center would be hard at work training the next generation of leaders to fight terrorists and other extremist groups. They are... except you might be very surprised at what the Pentagon is classifying as an "extremist" group.

According to a report by Todd Starnes, "The Department of Defense classified Catholics and Evangelical Christians as religious extremists similar to Al-Qaeda, according to training materials obtained by the Chaplain Alliance for Religious Liberty."

The revelations come just days after Judicial Watch discovered a separate Pentagon training document that depicted the Founding Fathers as extremists and conservative organizations as hate groups.

Chaplain Alliance uncovered in more than 1,500 pages of documents obtained through a Freedom of Information Act request after a U.S. Army training instructor told a Reserve unit based in Pennsylvania that Catholicism, Evangelical Christianity, Al Qaeda, Hamas, Sunni Muslims, and the Ku Klux Klan were examples of extremism.

What is going on here? Why are these types of characterizations allowed in Barack Obama's Department of Defense?

The training manual, which was obtained by Judicial Watch, it is noted that "many extremists will talk of individual liberties, states' rights, and how to make the world a better place." Wow... does that sound extremist to you? The manual actually states that "the colonists who sought to free themselves from British rule" are an example of "extremist ideologies and movements."

And here's one thing to note: The military training manuals use the Southern Poverty Law Center (SPLC) as a reference! Are you kidding me? As Starnes reports in another column, the SPLC is "a leftwing organization that has a history of labeling conservative Christian organizations like the Family Research Council as 'hate groups.'"

"Men and women of faith who have served the military faithfully for centuries shouldn't be likened to those who have regularly threatened the peace and security of the United States," Ron Crews, executive director of the Chaplain Alliance, said. "The materials we have received verify that the military views the Southern Poverty Law Center as a reliable source for Equal Opportunity briefings."

With Al Qaeda continuing to plan attacks against America, what in the world is the Pentagon doing focusing on Christians and using the SPLC as a reference? Something is definitely going wrong with our government, and I guess by saying that, I will now be labeled an extremist. Oh well.

If Noah had not built the Ark of Safety prior to the flood he and his entire household would have been drowned. If Joseph had not of stored up grain in Egypt prior to the seven years of famine, he and his entire household would have starved.

Our God knows what the future holds for this world. He is now calling out to his people through his prophets to prepare for the coming storm. Stop living your lives like it's never going to come. It must come for Christ to return to the earth to set up his kingdom.

The most important thing we can do now is to preserve truth. We have to stop our children and grandchildren from becoming indoctrinated with the government's socialist doctrines and agendas. We have to keep teaching them the truth of God's word and American values. We have to protect and guard their minds and the minds of God's people by preparing for them places of safety and protection where they can be taught the truth about the last days and Satan's great End-Time deceptions. If we don't we are going to lose our children to the government and to the Anti-christ as they will grow up only understanding socialist values.

If our kids remain in the school systems within 20 years (if the Lord tarry's) we will have lost them and they will be ripe to agree with and welcome the Anti-christ as God. They will feel proud to wear his mark showing their allegiance to him on their hand or forehead and they will feel like it is their duty to turn into the government anyone they find that does not have the mark, even if it's their parents.

Pray to the Lord for the Holy Spirit to guide you to one of his End-Time safety shelters.

We must do it now! If you wait until the storm hits it will be too late to prepare!

Get self-employed; buy land in the country with a stream and water supply. Store up commodities. Join with other born again Christians who are aware of the coming storm and begin to form communities of support.

But whenever these things begin to happen, take heart and lift up your heads, because your salvation draws near." (Luke 21:28 AB)

God is raising up "Goshen's" all over the world to protect his people in, try to locate one and get involved with it.

12

JUDGEMENT BEGINS IN THE HOUSE OF THE LORD

Where does judgment begin for all of the things that has happened in America? It begins with the Church that was designed to hold at bay the forces of darkness, being the demons and devils.

The Church has failed its great assignment! The Church has become intoxicated with the world and has become a lover of the world more than lovers of God. She has lost her power and sits an entity no different from the world with no real power or answers to offer anyone. The world that once turned to her for healing, comfort and resolution now just sits and laughs at her. She is a has-been. She talks of days gone by when the power of God moved mightily but she has no real power today. The world has gotten wise to her and wants no part of her. Her own members want no part of her and have pulled away creating the "Emergent Church Movement" because they know she has fallen, is not working, and has nothing to offer. She cannot even get a headache healed much less cancer or some fatal disease. She is powerless, and empty.

So the children of this world are turning to Hollywood for their role models, the TV and the internet to define them.

When I speak of the Church, I speak of it as a whole, I know there is always a "remnant" that God has out there that are walking holy and with their God. God will always have his remnant even though the number is small in comparison to this ungodly world.

Jesus said that when he returns to earth the Church will be in a "Laodicea State".

To the angel of the church in Laodicea write:

These are the words of the Amen, the faithful and true witness, the ruler of God's creation. I know your deeds, that you are neither cold nor hot. I wish you were either one or the other! So, because you are lukewarm—neither hot nor cold—I am about to spit you out of my mouth. You say, 'I am rich; I have acquired wealth and do not need a thing.' But you do not realize that you are wretched, pitiful, poor, blind and naked. I counsel you to buy from me gold refined in the fire, so you can become rich; and white clothes to wear, so you can cover your shameful nakedness; and salve to put on your eyes, so you can see. Those whom I love I rebuke and discipline. So be earnest and repent. Here I am! I stand at the door and knock. If anyone hears my voice and opens the door, I will come in and eat with that person, and they with me.

Jesus said the End-Time Church won't even have him inside. He will be standing on the outside knocking, pleading to come inside. Jesus said she would have the following qualities:

1.   She will not be led by the Holy Spirit- Jesus is standing on the outside

2.   She will be deceived: She thinks she's rich and satisfied and has need of nothing

3.   Her deeds are compromised: I know your deeds that you are neither cold nor hot

4.   She is wretched

191

5.   She is pitiful

6.   She is blind

7.   She is naked

Jesus's solution:

1.   Be cold or hot: get in or get out!

2.   Purchase gold that has been refined in the fire-bring the flesh under subjection to the Holy Spirit.

3.   Eye salve so she can see. Shake off the devils deception

4.   Purchase white clothes-put on holiness

5.   Be earnest and repent

6.   Hear his voice and open the door to him

The American Church is "satisfied". She is fat. She is full. She has her cake and is eating it too! She is going to church on Sundays to worship the Lord, then living like the world the rest of the week. Her lifestyle and activities are no different than the world. She goes to all of the world's entertainments and indulges herself in every form of pleasure that she can. She calls herself a Christian and believes that she is God-centered when in essence she is God-less and self-centered indulging her flesh in anything and everything that it wants from food, to recreational activities. She goes to country and worldly music concerts, wine tasting, and Las Vegas gambling. She watches the most popular television programs and fills her mind with the things of the world.

She is serving the "American Jesus". This is a Jesus that lives to serve and to please her instead of the other way around. It is a Jesus that has no "absolutes".

She is at liberty to partake in the world and serve Jesus too.

She is so full of carnality and the self that she is blinded to the things of God. They are foreign to her. If she does see someone that is walking in the Spirit she thinks they are weird or off balance.

She is lukewarm because she is a mixture of the flesh and the Spirit. She is both. Jesus said she is no good to either side that way.

She is blinded to the deep things of God and does not feel and know his heart for the End-Time's. Some of the things she indulges in are not necessarily wrong in themselves, but the closer you get to Jesus; you just lose your desire for them. They no longer appeal to you and instead of her losing her desire for worldly entertainment she wants more and more of it to the exclusion of spiritual things.

She is not clothed in humility or holiness thereby she is naked to the things of God and void of his discernment.

How did the Church get this way? She got this way because our Christian Fathers failed to teach us the right way. They failed to teach us that getting saved or born again is only the first step. They failed to teach us that after we are born again we have to allow the Holy Spirit who now lives inside of our spirits to break forth into our souls being our mind, will, and emotions and to take control of them. They failed to show us how to do this. They failed to teach us how to keep the flesh under subjection to the Holy Spirit and to walk in truth, love, and power.

We have accepted Jesus as savior but not as Lord. We have not been taught how to lay down our will, emotions, and minds to the Spirit of God so he can fill them with God's love and live his life through them.

When a Christian lives in control of their own emotions and mind they live no different from the world. This puts them into a position of allowing evil spirits to speak to their minds and to influence them. It allows for bondages to control their minds and emotions.

The Church is wounded. She is broken. This has caused the men of God who are our leaders to fall into every kind of sin imaginable. The world watched them fall and wants no part of our so called "Christianity". Anytime you live in the flesh instead of the spirit you will fail and succumb to sin. They yielded to fame, fortune, glamor, money, power and sexual perversion.

Ted Haggard:

Ted Haggard was the former leader of The National Association of Evangelicals. For three years he paid his masseur to have sex with him. During sex Haggard also consumed crystal meth. Haggard admitted buying the drugs and receiving massages from the masseur. In 2009 officials from Haggard's church announced that a young male church member had come forward in 2006 with "overwhelming pool of evidence of an inappropriate, consensual sexual relationship that went on for a long period of time.

Earl Paulk:

He also founded Cathedral at Chapel Hill, one of first American mega churches. He was accused sexually manipulating a woman in his congregation; and molesting a 7 year old girl.

Eddie L. Long:

In September 2010 four men filed separate lawsuits against Eddie Long, alleging him of using his influence to get them into having sex with him.

Paul Crouch:

Paul Franklin Crouch is a religious broadcaster and co-founder of the Trinity Broadcasting Network. In September 2004 LA Times published a report that in 1988 Crouch had paid a former employee $425,000 settlement to end a wrongful termination lawsuit which alleged homosexual encounters between Crouch and the person that got fired.

Jimmy Swaggart:

He was caught on two occasions with female prostitutes, once in 1988 and again in 1991. In the first instance, said prostitute revealed that Swaggart had expressed interest in her 13 year old daughter.

Kathryn Kullman:

Kathryn Kullman was a famous evangelist and faith healer. In 1935, Kathryn met Burroughs Waltrip, a Texas evangelist who was eight years her senior. Shortly after his visit to Denver, Waltrip divorced his wife, left his family and moved to Mason City, Iowa, where he began a revival center called Radio Chapel. Kathryn and her friend and pianist Helen Gulliford came into town to help him raise funds for his ministry. It was shortly after their arrival that the romance between Burroughs and Kathryn became publicly known.

A.A. Allen:

A. A. Allen was an evangelist with a Pentecostal healing and deliverance ministry. He was, for a time, associated with the "Voice of Healing" movement founded by Gordon Lindsay.

Allen died at the Jack Tar Hotel in San Francisco, California on June 11, 1970, at the age of 59. Allen died after a heavy drinking binge. Don Stewart, his successor, is said to have "attempted to clean up evidence of his mentor's alcoholic binge in a San Francisco hotel before the police arrived." Stewart says he wasn't trying to cover up anything, but was trying to protect Allen. Nonetheless, the claim is made that police found his body in a "room strewn with pills and empty liquor bottles." Following a 12-day investigation and an autopsy, the coroner's report concluded Allen died from liver failure brought on by acute alcoholism. The coroner reported that when Allen died he had a blood alcohol content of .36, which was "enough to ensure a deep coma". Allen was buried at Miracle Valley, Arizona on June 15, 1970.

Aimee Semple McPherson:

Aimee Semple McPherson was an, evangelist and media celebrity in the 1920s and 1930s. She founded the Foursquare Church.

On May 18, 1926, McPherson went with her secretary to Ocean Park Beach north of Venice Beach to swim. Soon after arriving, McPherson was nowhere to be found. It was thought she had drowned. It was later confirmed that she had been hid out with her boyfriend having an affair. Five witnesses who asserted to have seen McPherson at a seaside cottage in Carmel-by-the-Sea. She died in 1944 from an overdose of barbiturates.

And the list goes on and on of Christian ministers, evangelists, pastors and teachers who yielded to the flesh and were caught in scandals and debauchery bringing shame to the name of the Christ.

The youth of America has watched over and over again as these professing men and women of God have fallen from grace bringing shame upon themselves and the Church and they no longer want any part of it!

Not only do the people of America want no part of the Church, but they are actually blaming the Church for America's woes! The Christians and the Right are being named the "Terrorist's and the Haters".

The Laodicea Church is blind. She cannot see the state she is actually in. She calls wrong right and right wrong.

We need pastors and teachers who will rise up and teach us how to deny the flesh and to walk in the Spirit.

This is the only way true Christianity will be displayed to America. As long as the Church walks in the flesh she will falter and fail and be powerless and empty. Her nakedness appears to everyone except her. She thinks she is just fine! She thinks "Oh, well, we are all just human and we are going to make mistakes" so she overlooks her yielding's to the flesh. This teaching is so very, very, wrong. God did not send his son Jesus to this earth to give us a 'halfway" salvation. He came to make the way for us to be totally transformed into the image of his dear son. We just have to be taught how to do this. The sad thing is that America does not want to hear this kind of preaching. They do not want their sins exposed. They are happy and comfortable living in a luke-warm state.

The Church has failed America and has become a mixture of good and bad. She is lukewarm. She has lost her power to influence America to the things of God. America has turned to other religions or no religion at all looking for the answers she desperately seeks. We are no longer a Christian nation. We have been outnumbered by every other religion.

Our great men and women of God have failed to totally surrender themselves unto God. They have kept back enough of the flesh to do things their own way and to serve themselves. They love the money, the power, the fame, and the prestige. This has led to the down fall of the American culture. America is in a fallen state and now wants no part of God. Instead of teaching God's people how to be prepared for the End-Times the Church is preaching the "prosperity message" and teaching us how to be rich and enjoy our rewards here and now with no thought for what's about to happen. Just look at their homes, tailor made clothes, cars and airplanes.

13

SATAN HAS DECEIVED THE CHURCH

Don't be sitting there thinking, "Satan cannot deceive the Church", well just think about this: he deceived Eve! And she was in the "state of perfection". She was far more perfect than you and I and Christians are today!

The Apostle Paul tried so hard to teach the Church of his day the truth of God's word, but Satan has come along and gained a foot hold into the Church by deceiving it into believing the very things that Paul warned them not to believe or to be deceived about.

Satan has gained large ground and is laughing at us because we all bought one of his greatest deceptions. It is regarding the last days.

Satan has deceived the Church and caused her to be off of her guard, unconcerned and unprepared for the last days because he has tricked her into believing that she will not be here but be taken away in a secret "rapture". This has caused her to be totally unprepared spiritually, emotionally, and physically and mentally for the coming hard days just ahead.

When they do hit and the Church sees that they have been taught wrong from their pastors, there will be a great falling away of God's people from discouragement and lack of belief in anything about religion.

The people will turn from believing in God at all because they will realize that the things they had been taught were not true, so they will doubt if anything they were ever taught about God was true, and they will turn and follow the greatest deception of all, being the Antichrist.

The Pastors of our churches say, oh I am not concerned about "End-Time events", I am just teaching the people how to live for Christ each day. This is such nonsense because what they are actually saying is that they believe they will be raptured out of here and there is no need to be that concerned about End-Time events.

If these pastors truly had the heartbeat of God they would definitely be concerned because that is what is on his heart. He is getting ready to bring his Kingdom down to earth. This is what is on the heart of God. The Pastors cannot hear the heartbeat of the Lord or they would be greatly concerned for what he is doing in the earth and what he is concerned about. They would be crying to the Lord, "Break my heart for what breaks yours!"

This deception about the secret rapture was one of Satan's greatest accomplishments against the Church, and she bought into it hook, line, and sinker.

I believed it most of my whole life too because I had been taught it by my teachers and leaders, but when God called me to be an "End-Time Prophet", he began to reveal to me this great deception and commanded me to teach his people the truth, even though most won't be able to receive it, because it's very hard to stop believing what you think is the "truth", and people think, well if most of the people believe this way it has to be right.

This teaching has left the Church sitting ducks for the coming hard times.

The pastors of our churches should be teaching us how to deal with it emotionally when we see our loved ones beheaded or martyred and how to have enough strength to not take the Mark of the Beast no matter what. They should be teaching us mentally all of the things to be looking for that are about to happen so we are not caught off guard or live in fear. They should be teaching us to stock up food and commodities and to feed ourselves and our loved ones. They should be teaching us about our great King's return to overtake the kingdoms of this earth and to set up his kingdom, so we can be praying in unison with the Holy Spirit. They should be teaching us how to be prepared so we can help others and win souls to God during this hard time.

But the things they are teaching us are that the church age ends at the fourth chapter of Revelations and we get secretly raptured out and the rest of the whole book of Revelations is not for the Church at all but for the Jews (even though Jesus told John to write the whole book to the seven churches) . This has left the Church unconcerned about End-Time events, unprepared for them, and off guard about them.

Satan does not want the Church to be a mighty force against him during the time of his greatest feat which is his empowering of the Man of Sin, the Anti-christ. He has been successful in causing his greatest enemy, which is the Church to be unprepared as a whole to be a target against him, but what he has forgotten is that God always keeps himself a remnant that are walking close enough to him to hear his heartbeat and to know his plans and purposes in the earth, and this remnant is going to rise up against him. The Bible says that the people who do know their God will rise up and do exploits for him in the last days. (Dan. 11:32)

We have been deceived Church! It is as simple as that! Christ warned us that in the last days what we needed to watch out for was deception!

Jesus gave us seven churches in the book of Revelation that he sent letters to. These seven churches were actual, living churches at that time. They also represented seven different church ages down through history. The last church was the Church of Laodicea which Christ accused of being arrogant and thinking they had it all together and had need of nothing. (They would be serving the American Jesus) They thought they were right! But Christ says you don't even know that you are blind! This is the church of today! We think we have it all together and that we know everything, when Christ says we are lukewarm, poor, blind, and miserable! And know nothing as we ought to know!

I know your deeds, that you are neither cold nor hot. I wish you were either one or the other! So, because you are lukewarm—neither hot nor cold—I am about to spit you out of my mouth. You say, 'I am rich; I have acquired wealth and do not need a thing.' But you do not realize that you are wretched, pitiful, poor, blind and naked. I counsel you to buy from me gold refined in the fire, so you can become rich; and white clothes to wear, so you can cover your shameful nakedness; and salve to put on your eyes, so you can see.

Those whom I love I rebuke and discipline. So be earnest and repent. (Rev. 3:15)

The church of today in general is serving "The American Jesus", and is blinded by Satan concerning End-Time events. The Church is so self-absorbed and proud that it is near impossible to wake her up to the truth of God's word and her spiritual condition.

Jesus says that she is wretched, pitiful, and poor. This is because we have not been taught about how to allow the Holy Spirit that resides within our spirits to flow into our souls. We haven't been taught that when we get saved only our spirits are born again, and that our souls do not change and have to be transformed by the Spirit of God on a daily basis, so the Church in general is serving God out of their soulish realm and they live and act not much different from the world because they have not been taught how to lay down the flesh and walk in the Spirit. (Please read my two books to gain power over this condition. "There is a River", and "Let the River Flow". Both can be obtained at Amazon.com)

The second thing he said was that she was blind and naked. This is because Satan has blinded her mind and she is naked to the truth of God's word. She thinks she is ok when she actually is in a very dangerous condition.

This is the church that I am addressing and begging and pleading with to wake up from your sleep and slumber. Shake off the false teachings of Satan that has deceived you. Learn how to be led and guided by the Holy Spirit and to truly become a new creation in Christ, not a mixture of self and Christ. The Church of today is a mutant, unable to help herself much less anyone else. She is a mixture of Christ and the world. She is walking around like a Zombie, not fully dead and not fully alive.

Please prayerfully listen as I teach you the truth of what Apostle Paul taught us. Listen to my teaching without your preconceived beliefs, false teachings, and arrogant belief that you already know the whole truth. We will take it verse by verse.

Now, dear brothers and sisters let us clarify some things about the coming of our Lord Jesus Christ and how we will be gathered to meet him. (2 Thess.2:1 NIV)

Apostle Paul wanted so badly to clarify to the Church the things concerning the Rapture of the Church. There were already false teachings going around.

Don't be so easily shaken or alarmed by those who say that the day of the Lord has already begun. Don't believe them, even if they claim to have had a spiritual vision, a revelation, or a letter supposedly from us. (2 Thess. 2:2 NIV)

Don't be fooled by what they say. For that day will not come until there is a great rebellion against God and the man of lawlessness is revealed—the one who brings destruction. (2 Thess. 2:3)

The first thing Paul was trying to teach them is that the teaching of "eminence" regarding the coming of the Lord was false. The teaching of eminence says that the Rapture can happen at any time. Paul says "Don't be fooled by what they say, the Rapture will not come immediately!

Paul was also prophesying about the future when he said "don't believe this false teaching even if someone claims to have a spiritual vision or revelation about it, and that is exactly what did happen in the 1800's and the Church fell for it and still believes it and teaches it today!

There is no mention of a pre-tribulation or a mid-tribulation Rapture in any Church teaching, writing or commentary until the early 1800s when the pre-tribulation Rapture heresy began.

In 1812, a Jesuit priest from Chile, South America named Manuel de Lacunza, writing under the pen-name of Rabbi J.J. Ben-Ezra, wrote a book called "The Coming of the Messiah in Glory and Majesty."

In his book, he set forth the idea that the Rapture and the Second Coming of Jesus will be separated by a period of time. He claimed that all of the other Church teachers and leaders up to 1812 had been wrong in teaching a post-tribulation Rapture. He basically said that he was right; and they had all been "convicted of error" in their teaching.

Edward Irving, a Scottish preacher, translated de Lacunza's book from Spanish into English and had it published in London in 1827. Around that time, Irving began to preach that there would be a pre-tribulation Rapture of the Church.

Margaret MacDonald in the town of Port Glasgow, Scotland catapulted this heresy. Supposedly in 1830 she had a dream or vision that Christians were raptured just prior to the Great Tribulation. John Nelson Darby, the founder of a group known as the Plymouth Brethren, after visiting Miss MacDonald began teaching this new theory.

Later, by 1917, C. I. Scofield had published his improved edition of the Scofield Reference Bible which contained the dispensational pre-tribulation teachings of Darby and others. Soon many Bible Colleges such as Moody Bible Institute and seminaries such as Dallas

Theological Seminary became staunch promoters of dispensational theology that included the doctrine of a pre-tribulation rapture.

Hal Lindsey popularized this teaching with his book titled The Late Great Planet Earth. Several million copies have been sold and a movie by the same title was made. So this false teaching has become the most popular Christian world view, but just because it is popular doesn't make it right!

If a church has a huge congregation that doesn't necessarily mean the church is Spirit filled, and just because the majority of the modern day Christians believes this heresy, doesn't mean it is the truth! We cannot escape the importance of the writings of the early Church fathers, especially those prior to the First Council of Nicaea in A.D.325, heavily influenced by the oral tradition of the apostolic teachings. It is, therefore, important to recognize that these men all held to a historic pre-millennial view, in which the concept of a pre-tribulation resurrection-"rapture" of church only saints was inconceivable to them.

It was not until the mid-nineteenth century when a Triad of elitist Plymouth Brethren members, John Nelson Darby, Cyrus Scofield, and Sir Robert Anderson, invented, introduced, and promoted the doctrine of Dispensationalism, which is the source of the pre-tribulation resurrection-"rapture" of church only saints. But one thing is certain; if the dispensational doctrine of a pre-tribulation resurrection-"rapture" of church only saints had surfaced in earlier days, it would have been universally exposed as heresy.

Are we, therefore, really going to accept this new theory without a thorough, Spirit-guided exegesis when ALL of the church fathers prior to this time, including John the Apostle, taught that the church would be persecuted by the Antichrist and that there would only be one resurrection of the righteous, which would take place on the "last day"?

Pre-Nicene Council

Justin Martyr (A.D. 100-168):

Two advents of Christ have been announced: the one, in which He is set forth as suffering, inglorious, dishonored, and crucified; but the other, in which He shall come from heaven with glory, when the man of apostasy, who speaks strange things against the Most High, shall venture to do unlawful deeds on the earth against us the Christians. (First Apology of Justine, Chapter 110)

Irenaeus (A.D. 140-202), student of Polycarp taught by the apostle, John:

And then he... (Daniel)...points out the time that his tyranny shall last, during which the

Saints shall be put to flight. (Against Heresies V, XXVL, 1) And they shall lay Babylon waste, and burn her with fire, and shall give their kingdom to the beast, and put the Church to flight. (Against Heresies V, XXVI)

Tertullian (A.D. 160-220):

That the beast Antichrist, with his false prophet, may wage war on the Church of God. (On the Resurrection of the Flesh, 25)

Cyprian (A.D. 200-258):

The Lord hath foretold that these things would come. With the exhortation of His foreseeing word, instructing, and teaching, and preparing, and strengthening the people of His Church for all endurance of things to come. He previously warned us that the adversary would increase more and more in the last times. (Treatise 7)

For you ought to know and to believe, and hold it for certain, that the day of affliction has begun to hang over our heads, and the end of the world and the time of Antichrist to draw near, so that we must all stand prepared for the battle...The time cometh, that whosoever killeth you will think that he doeth God service...Nor let any one wonder that we are harassed with increasing afflictions, when the Lord before predicted that these things would happen in the last times.

(Epistles of Cyprian, LV, 1, 2)

Nor let any one of you, beloved brethren, be so terrified by the fear of future persecution, or the coming of the threatening Antichrist, as not to be found armed for all things by the evangelical exhortations and precepts, and by the heavenly warnings. (Cyprian, LIII, p.722)

Hippolytus (A.D. 160-240):

213

...the one thousand two hundred and three score days (the half of the week) during which

the tyrant is to reign and persecute the Church... (Treatise on Christ and Antichrist, 61)

Victorinus of Poetovia (? -303)

The little season signifies three years and six months, in which with all his power the devil will avenge himself under Antichrist against the Church. (Commentary on the Apocalypse, 20:1-3)

Post-Nicene Council

Augustine (A.D. 354-430):

...the kingdom of Antichrist shall fiercely, though for a short time, assail the Church... (The City of God, XX, 3)

Roger Bacon (A.D. 1214-1274):

...future perils [for the Church] in the times of Antichrist... (Opus Majus II, page 634)

Martin Luther (A.D. 1483-1546):

[The book of Revelation] is intended as a revelation of things that are to happen in the future, and especially of tribulations and disasters for the Church... (Works of Martin Luther, VI, p. 481)

John Knox (A.D. 1515-1572):

The great love of God towards his Church, whom he pleased to forewarn of dangers to come...to wit, the man of sin, The Antichrist... (The History of the Reformation etc., I, p.76)

Roger Williams (A.D. 1603-1683):

Antichrist...hath his prisons, to keep Christ Jesus and his members fast. (The Bloody Tenent etc., p. 153)

Charles Hodge (A.D. 1797-1878):

...the fate of his Church here on earth...is the burden of the Apocalypse. (Systematic Theology, III, p. 827)

Carl F. Keil (A.D. 1807-1888):

...the persecution of the last enemy Antichrist against the Church of the Lord... (Biblical Commentary, YXMV, 503)

He says don't let others tell you that the Rapture can happen at any time. He says "That day" meaning the day of the Rapture will not come immediately, two things must happen first!

Don't be fooled by what they say. For that day will not come until there is a great rebellion against God and the man of lawlessness is revealed—the one who brings destruction. (2 Thess. 2:3).

Don't be fooled, was the Apostle Paul's warning! The Rapture will not come until two things happen first.

1.   A great falling away of God's people

2.   The Anti-Christ is revealed

I just cannot understand how anyone cannot understand those verses! How much clearer does Paul have to be? He teaches the Rapture of the Church will not come until we see two things happen first. This refutes the false teaching of imminence, and of a secret rapture! The actual great falling away of God's people will be caused in large by this false teaching because they will realize they were taught wrong by the very ones that they looked up to admired, and respected and when they find themselves in a precarious situation they will be unprepared to face it so they will take the Mark of the Beast to try to survive.

The teaching of a pre-tribulation secret Rapture of the Church is one of the most deadly things that has ever happened to the Church.

He will exalt himself and defy everything that people call god and every object of worship. He will even sit in the temple of God, claiming that he himself is God. (2. Thess.2:4 NLT)

Don't you remember that I told you about all this when I was with you? (2. The 2:5)

The Apostle Paul was saying that he had thought it very important and had taught them all about the coming Anti-christ when he had been with them. If he did not think the Church would see the Anti-christ he would not have taken the time to teach them about him. Come on Saints! Wake up!

And you know what is holding him back, for he can be revealed only when his time comes. (2 Thess. 2:6 NLT)

For this lawlessness is already at work secretly, and it will remain secret until the one who is holding it back steps out of the way. (2. Thess. 2:7 NIV)

These two verses here verse 6 and 7 are the verses that have been falsely taught that teach something so absurd that I do not understand how a sane person could possible believe it.

This false teaching teaches that the "restrainer" is the Holy Spirit and when he takes the Church off the earth in the secret rapture he will be gone and then the Anti-christ can be revealed because he is not here to restrain him any longer.

First of all, these scriptures make absolutely no mention of the Holy Spirit being the restrainer at all, and there is absolutely no other scripture in the entire bible that correlates to this teaching. There is however another scripture that plainly teaches you who and what this restrainer is as it tells us as plain as day! So let me first ask you this. Do you want to continue to believe a doctrine that there is no scripture to sustain or do you want to believe what the Bible states? That is my first question to you. If you do not want to know what the Bible says then there is no reason for you to continue reading this book. If you want to know what the Bible says the restrainer is then I will tell you.

First let's look at who the beast is:

Now when they have finished their testimony, the beast that comes up from the Abyss will attack them, and overpower and kill them. (Rev. 11:7 NLV))

And when they shall have finished their testimony, the beast that ascendeth out of the bottomless pit shall make war against them, and shall overcome them, and kill them. (Rev. 11:7)

Where does the Beast come from? The bottomless pit!

What is the restrainer of the Anti-christ? The bottomless pit where he is in prison! Who releases him and is taken away so he can be revealed? The angel of the Lord by removing his chains and opening up the locked door to the Abyss!

The fifth angel sounded his trumpet, and I saw a star that had fallen from the sky to the earth. The star was given the key to the shaft of the Abyss. When he opened the Abyss, smoke rose from it like the smoke from a gigantic furnace. The sun and sky were darkened by the smoke from the Abyss. And out of the smoke locusts came down on the earth and were given power like that of scorpions of the earth. They were told not to harm the grass of the earth or any plant or tree, but only those people who did not have the seal of God on their foreheads. They were not allowed to kill them but only to torture them for five months. And the agony they suffered was like that of the sting of a scorpion when it strikes. During those days people will seek death but will not find it; they will long to die, but death will elude them.

The locusts looked like horses prepared for battle. On their heads they wore something like crowns of gold, and their faces resembled human faces. Their hair was like women's hair, and their teeth were like lions' teeth. They had breastplates like breastplates of iron, and the sound of their wings was like the thundering of many horses and chariots rushing into battle. They had tails with stingers, like scorpions, and in their tails they had power to torment people for five months.

They had as king over them the angel of the Abyss, whose name in Hebrew is Abaddon and in Greek is Apollyon (that is, Destroyer).

The angel unlocks the bottomless pit which is the restrainer of the Anti-christ. The demon spirit which is the called Abaddon or Apollyon will come up out of the bottomless pit and enter into a man and possess him and bring him back to life. He will be released along with a great army of demons who will come upon the earth to do his bidding.

This demon will be given his great power from Satan. There will an unholy trinity.

Satan will act as father God behind the scenes, the Anti-christ as Satan's son alive upon the earth, and the false prophet as the Holy Spirit. They will all three imitate the real Holy Trinity and try to conquer heaven and earth.

Then the man of lawlessness will be revealed, but the Lord Jesus will kill him with the breath of his mouth and destroy him by the splendor of his coming. (2 Thess. 2:8)

This man will come to do the work of Satan with counterfeit power and signs and miracles. (2. Thess. 2:9)

He will use every kind of evil deception to fool those on their way to destruction, because they refuse to love and accept the truth that would save them. (2. Thess. 2:10)

So God will cause them to be greatly deceived, and they will believe these lies. (2. Thess. 2:11)

Then they will be condemned for enjoying evil rather than believing the truth. (2 Thess. 2:12NLT)

Don't be fooled by what they say. For that day will not come until there is a great rebellion against God and the man of lawlessness is revealed—the one who brings destruction. (2 Thess. 2:3).

Don't be fooled, was the Apostle Paul's warning! The Rapture will not come until two things happen first.

1.   A great falling away of God's people

2.   The Anti-christ is revealed

We need to understand who and what the Holy Spirit is. The Holy Spirit is the third person of the Holy Trinity. He came down to earth to do the following:

Convict the heart of sin. (John 16:8)

Live inside of the believer to lead and guide them. (John 14:17)

There is absolutely no scripture that says he came down to earth to fight any outside forces. Jesus said he was sending him to us from the Father so he could live on the inside of us and comfort us.

It is the wrong interpretation of scripture to say that the Holy Spirit fights any outside forces, or that he came to earth to be any kind of restrainer. There are no scriptures that ever say this. He cannot hold back the Anti-christ from being revealed because he only works on the inside of believers.

There are however many scriptures that say the angels of God come down to earth to fight and hold back the forces of darkness. (Dan. 10:13)

If you are not sure what a scripture means, then you have to look elsewhere in the Bible to find out. It is the angel that comes down to earth that opens up the Abyss so the demon king can come out onto the world.

The angel and the gate to the bottomless pit are the restrainers of the Anti-christ.

To say that the Holy Spirit is the restrainer of the Anti-christ because when he takes the Church to heaven in a secret rapture then there is no force left upon this earth to restrain him so he can come forth in his evil power is just absurd! Just look around you. Just study history. The Holy Spirit being upon this earth has never stopped sin and corruption. It didn't stop Hitler, it didn't stop Antiochus Epiphanes, and it won't stop the Anti-christ!

Our world grows more evil every day. There is no restrainer of evil here upon this earth. Evil is released by the choices of men, not by the Holy Spirit either allowing or not allowing it.

Also, it is because the Church has not been taught who and what the Holy Spirit truly is, that they have become susceptible to believing the lie about him being removed from the earth at the Rapture of the Church.

Let me explain to you: There are three separate individuals in heaven. They are all co-equal, co-eternal, and co- God. They all three are of the same essence and make up our Holy Godhead. Father God is a spirit being who has a body. He told Moses that he could see his back parts but not his face and live. He is the Ancient of Days. He sits upon his throne and rules this universe. Jesus Christ is God's son and our risen savior. He has a glorified body just like we will have. He sits on the right hand side of the Father in heaven. They both stay primarily in heaven, but it is the Holy Spirit that is the seven lamps of fire before the throne, and it is he that comes down to earth and is working in the lives of God's people. He is on the outside of us and the inside of us. The Holy Spirit is a spirit. He is everywhere at the same time. If you go to the highest mountain you will find him. If you go to the lowest ocean you will find him.

In Jeremiah 23:24 God declares, "Do I not fill heaven and earth? (Jer.23:24)

Whither shall I go from thy spirit? Or whither shall I flee from thy presence? If I ascend into heaven, thou art there: if I make my bed in hell, behold, thou art there. If I take the wings of the morning, and dwell in the uttermost parts of the sea; even there shall thy hand lead me, and thy right hand shall hold me" (Psalms 139:7-10)

He is the ears and eyes of the Lord. He is omnipresent. This means that he is everywhere at the same time.

If I ascend up into heaven, thou art there: if I make my bed in hell, behold, thou art there. (Ps. 139:8)

The eyes of the LORD are in every place, beholding the evil and the good. (Prov.15:3)

For his eyes are on the ways of man, and he sees all his goings. (Job 34:21)

Neither is there any creature that is not manifest in his sight. (Heb. 14:3)

So, then if you really believe the above scriptures, you can clearly see that it is impossible for someone or something that is omnipresent to leave any place.

The Holy Spirit cannot ever leave this world or any other place because he is a spirit that is everywhere at the same time.

The Holy Spirit does not restrain anybody, and he will never leave this earth. How do you think people can get saved during the tribulation if he is not here to convict their hearts? (Rev. 17:4)

The false teachings of the secret Rapture teaches that the Book of Revelation was written for primarily the Jewish people. It states that only the first four chapters are for the Church and when the saints are mentioned during the Tribulation it is referring to the Jews and other people who get save that is not the Church.

If this is the case, then God should not have ever put these following scripture into the Bible because I believe them:

There is neither Jew nor Greek, there is neither bond nor free, there is neither male nor female: for you are all one in Christ Jesus. (Gal. 3:28)

But a Jew is one inwardly, and circumcision is a matter of the heart, by the Spirit, not by the letter. His praise is not from man but from God. (Rom 2:29)

Boast not against the branches. But if thou boast, thou bearest not the root, but the root thee. Thou wilt say then, the branches were broken off, that I might be grafted in.

Well; because of unbelief they were broken off, and thou standest by faith. Be not high-minded, but fear. For if God spared not the natural branches, take heed lest he also spare not thee.

Behold therefore the goodness and severity of God: on them which fell, severity; but toward thee, goodness, if thou continue in his goodness: otherwise thou also shalt be cut off.

This mystery is that through the gospel the Gentiles are heirs together with Israel, members together of one body, and sharers together in the promise in Christ Jesus. (Eph3:6)

Saints we are not different from Israel. We have been grafted into the vine. Every person that has been born again is spiritual Israel.

Christ redeemed us from the curse of the Law, having become a curse for us for it is written, "Cursed is everyone who hangs on a tree" in order that in Christ Jesus the blessing of Abraham might come to the

Gentiles, so that we would receive the promise of the Spirit through faith. (Gal 3: 13)

Abraham is the father of the Jews, and he is our father as well. In Christ we receive the blessings of Abraham.

The Church did not replace Israel; the Church became a part of Israel. We were grafted in. We do not receive special blessings of a secret Rapture while the Jews remain here to endure the Great Tribulation.

Every person that is born again has become spiritual Israel and the Church, whether Gentile or Jew. There is no difference.

Father God does have special plans ahead for the nation of Israel. That is where he is going to rule the earth from, and he plans to save them as a nation as well.

Let me ask you this. Do you believe you are going to live in the New Jerusalem? Well just think about this: there are no gates into the city that say this gate is for the Church! All of the entrances to the city are named after the Jews! And we better be humble and thankful enough to Father God that he has made a way for us to enter into the Jewish gates, not to think that we hold some elite place above the Jews!

The saved of the earth are God's people, no matter what nationality they are, and they receive all of the blessings that God promised to Father Abraham. We have been grafted in!

Another scripture that this false teaching takes to try to sustain this false teaching is the fourth chapter of Revelation. First they teach that the Church is not mentioned after this chapter, but they are wrong, because it mentions the saints, and the elect, and God's people all through the rest of the book. Where they went wrong was to make a distinction between the Church and the Saints or God's elect.

Unto the church of God which is at Corinth, to them that are sanctified in Christ Jesus, called to be saints, with all that in every place call upon the name of Jesus Christ our Lord, both theirs and ours. (1 Cor. 1:2)

I don't know about you but I do believe that Paul was addressing the Church when he called them Saint's. So if indeed we are the Saints, when do we stop being the Saints at the Rapture?

And he shall speak great words against the most High, and shall wear out the saints of the most High, and think to change times and laws: and they shall be given into his hand until a time and times and the dividing of time. (Dan. 7:25)

This verse is talking about the Anti-christ and the Great Tribulation when the Anti-christ will wreak havoc on God's people for three and a half years.

Then the dragon became furious with the woman and went off to make war on the rest of her offspring, on those who keep the commandments of God and hold to the testimony of Jesus. And he stood on the sand of the sea. (Rev. 12:17)

The woman was Israel which the Church is grafted into. Surely you can see that her offspring would not be holding the testimony of Jesus Christ if these people were only the Jews, because the Jews hate Jesus Christ. The offspring is referring to every person alive that has been born again. It is not referring to the nation of Israel alone.

Paul, a servant of God, and an apostle of Jesus Christ, according to the faith of God's elect, and the acknowledging of the truth which is after godliness. (Titus 1:1)

Israel is not God's elect. Everyone that believes in Jesus Christ is God's elect.

In Revelation Chapter 4 it says: After these things I looked, and behold a door was opened in heaven, and the first voice which I heard was as it were of a trumpet talking with me which said, Come up hither, and I will shew thee things which must be hereafter.

Where did it say anything about a "Rapture of the Church?" The angel told John that he was going to catch him up to heaven to shew him the glory of father God so he would have a better understanding that the coming judgments were orchestrated by a loving, beautiful God who yearned with desire for his people and was about to drive evil off of this planet because he was bringing justice to his children.. If you don't first understand the heart of father God for his people then you can never truly understand the judgments and the destruction that is coming and the part we play in it.

I have been called up by the Holy Spirit many times to heaven and viewed the sea of glass and the throne room of Father God, but the rapture did not occur.

This teaching is purely assumption with no scriptural basis at all.

Then they say because they see the 24 elders around the throne that the rapture had to have just happened. Well they teach that because they have never been transported in the spirit up to God's throne, because those 24 elders are there right now, I have seen them!

The 24 Elders has been in the Throne Room of Father God making up the heavenly Sanhedrin and helping him rule his universe for a very long time. They are redeemed saints who are chosen and worthy to rule with him on his throne.

14

THE RAPTURE OF THE CHURCH

When does the Rapture of the Church occur? Well, let's take a look at scripture.

Listen, I tell you a mystery: We will not all sleep, but we will all be changed in a flash, in the twinkling of an eye, at the last trumpet, for the trumpet will sound, the dead will be raised imperishable, and we will be changed. For the perishable must clothe itself with the imperishable and the mortal with immortality. When the perishable has been clothed with the imperishable, and the mortal with immortality, then the saying that is written will come true: "Death has been swallowed up in victory. "Where, O death is your victory? Where, O death is your sting?" The sting of death is sin, and the power of sin is the law.

The first thing about this scripture is that right away this teaching takes it out of context. It says the "Mystery" is a secret Rapture. If you truly study the whole chapter you will see that the "Mystery" is that living Saints will not die, but will be clothed upon with immortality, and immortality will swallow up death. This is a great mystery and it has been provided for us in Christ.

The Apostle Paul says this event will happen "at the last trump". This statement of him is completely ignored in the false teaching. Paul didn't say "last" to just be talking. He said what he meant. The Rapture of the Church will happen at the last trump.

Every one of the Jew's knew what this meant. The last trump was always associated with the fall feast of trumpets. Paul is telling them that Christ would return at the last trump, which they knew to be a future "Feast of Trumpets". Jesus also verified this, when he told them that no man would know the day or the hour of his return, they knew perfectly well what he was saying. He also was telling them that he would return on a future feast of trumpets. The Feast of Trumpets was the only feast that no man could know the day or the hour it would begin because it would fall between a two day window when the full moon was spotted.

Both Paul and Jesus let the Church know that the Rapture would fall upon a future fall feast called the Feast of Trumpets. Paul also said it would be the last trump of the feast.

We find this substantiated in the Book of Revelations:

Then the seventh angel sounded: And there were loud voices in heaven, saying, "The kingdoms of this world have become the kingdoms of our Lord and of His

Christ, and He shall reign forever and ever!" And the twenty-four elders who sat before God on their thrones fell on their faces and worshiped God, saying:

"We give You thanks, O Lord God Almighty, The One who is and who was and who is to come, Because You have taken Your great power and reigned. The nations were angry, and your wrath has come, and the time of the dead, that they should be judged, And that You should reward your servants the prophets and the saints, and those who fear your name, small and great, and should destroy those who destroy the earth."

The time that the dead should be raised back up and all of God's servants receive their rewards is at the sounding of the last trumpet in Revelation on a future Feast of Trumpets.

This event will take place 30 days prior to the Battle of Armageddon when God's wrath will be poured out upon the world. We will be in heaven on the sea of glass receiving our rewards, then we will return to earth with Christ all riding upon white horses to the Battle of Armageddon where Christ will destroy all the wicked kingdoms of this world and set down his kingdom upon the earth and we shall rule and reign with him for a thousand years.

When did Jesus say he would return and rapture his Saints? "He said he would return on the last day" of human history.

For my Father's will is that everyone who looks to the Son and believes in him shall have eternal life, and I will raise him up at the last day (John 6:40).

There is no secret rapture prior to the last day. The Bible says the resurrection when Jesus returns at the end of the Great Tribulation is the First Resurrection, so how can there be one prior to that? First means First! Come on Saints wake up!

15

WORKING TOGETHER FOR THE COMMON GOOD

People in general are self-centered and possessive of their achievements and material things. Most Christian families will share with each other but never accept the idea of sharing or working together for a common goal with others.

We have a "God bless me and mine" attitude and everyone else can fend for themselves! Or if people do get together to share they are labeled a "cult" or weird.

Jesus made us a family and the Church has completely forgotten and lost its heritage. There is very little brotherly love flowing amongst us.

All the believers were one in heart and mind. No one claimed that any of their possessions was their own, but they shared everything they had. (Acts 4:32 NLT).

When I think of this and the way the early church was founded and I compare it to today there is no resemblance. Everyone had the same mind and heart. They loved each other. They cared for each other. They made sure each other had their needs met.

All the believers were one in heart and mind. No one claimed that any of their possessions was their own, but they shared everything they had. With great power the apostles continued to testify to the resurrection of the Lord Jesus. And God's grace was so powerfully at work in them all. There were no needy persons among them. For from time to time those who owned land or houses sold them, brought the money from the sales and put it at the apostles' feet, and it was distributed to anyone who had need. (Acts 4:32-35NIV)

There was not one needy person among them!

This is how true Christianity works! This is how true love works! It is not selfish but kind and giving. They were filled with the love of God and they ministered to each other.

God is love and he desires a people who are filled with his love. His first commandment is:

He answered, "'Love the Lord your God with all your heart and with all your soul and with all your strength and with all your mind'; and, 'Love your neighbor as yourself.'"(Lk 10:27 NIV)

So, why can't we do this? It is because we are not walking in the Holy Spirit; we are walking and living in the flesh realm of our wounded souls. This is why there has been so much trouble in the Churches and why the church is in a Laodicea Luke warm state.

The first thing that needs to happen within the Church is that they need to be taught how to deny the flesh, crucify it and how to live their lives in the Holy Spirit. This is a very hard teaching and there are not many today that want to hear this much less do this. They are happy and satisfied living in the flesh because they can have their own way and please themselves.

Satan has robbed the Church of this teaching. It is the greatest weapon against him. When a person walks in the Spirit his weapons cannot penetrate and hurt them. They just bounce off and he loses control.

The Church is carnal and fleshly and they do not know how to be any other way. They pray and speak in tongues on Sunday and cuss their husband, wife or a neighbor out on Monday. Until the Church learns how to die so they can live there will be no real power or victory in it and God cannot and will not pour his Spirit out upon it in a great way.

So the first thing we need are good teachers who can walk us through how to crucify the flesh and how to get and stay filled with the Holy Spirit.

The things that we are about to face will defeat us if we don't learn how to do this. It's only when our minds have been renewed and our hearts are full of love, peace, and hope that we will be able to face the hard times without giving into the Mark of the Beast. So many Christians are going to fall because they are hungry and they don't know how to deny their flesh.

So the very first thing we need is to be taught how to deny the flesh and yield to the Holy Spirit.

Second, we need to be taught how to endure persecution, and how to stand without giving in to the Mark of the Beast. We need to be taught how to endure when we see a loved one tortured or murdered.

Third, we need to be taught about world events and Biblical events so when they happen we will not be afraid but we will understand the heart and plans of our heavenly father.

Fourth, we need to begin to create communities where we gather as a group and all contribute for the common good. We need to get out of the cities and learn to live off of the grid so when the grid goes down we are not devastated but we can take care of ourselves. We need to get away from the coastal areas as they will be covered by tsunamis. We need to gather as groups and live together in the mountains. But most important is to be led by the Holy Spirit as to where in the mountains. Some places are divinely protected by God and nothing will be able to penetrate to harm you during the tribulation not even the government or the Anti-christ.

Church, please listen to me. I speak to you as a prophet of the Lord. Now is the time to prepare. We don't have much time left. We need to be taught. We need to be filled with the Holy Spirit. We need to prepare commodities and store up water, food, and medicines. We need to each contribute time, talents, and finances for the common good.

The thing that breaks my heart is that I know that most of the Church will not heed this warning and they will continue to live like they are half in the spirit and half in the world. They will not prepare and when this all hits they will be the ones who are rounded up and slaughtered, or they will be the ones who succumb and take the Mark of the Beast.

The ones who listen now and prepare will be hidden away in safety by the Lord until the storm passes by. The angel of the Lord will fight for you and defend you.

The Lord has commissioned me to open up a place here in Louisiana where people can gather together. We will meet for the first time on Saturday Jan.4th, 2014. The first goal is to teach and prepare them to crucify the flesh and be filled with the Holy Spirit. This is the first priority and the most important thing of all.

We will discuss ways of storing up commodities and preparing for the apocalypse. We will gather people here in the Denham Springs, area of Louisiana, but we will buy land up in the mountains in the Ozarks and we will send people up there to create a refuge for us all to run to when things get really bad and Marshall Law is declared. We can all go up there and take turns working in it when we can get up there and it will contain a large storage facility where we will store up 7 years' worth of food, water, and medicine for each other. We will build an underground safety bunker to enter into and lock the door when the Lord says it's time to enter into it.

We will all work together for the good of ourselves, our families and our friends. We will have open doors for as many Christians as God sends to us to protect. We are not a "Survivalists Group" with guns and ammunition that horde food and don't share it. We are a group of Christians who are going before God's people making a way of protection and provision for all as Joseph was sent into Egypt to feed the whole land of Egypt when the famine hit.

We do not have much time left. Obama is working as fast as he can to disarm the American people of their weapons and to bring about a police state and to imprison all Christians under the guise of being terrorists.

Our school system is already compromised and communism is being taught to our children. We must remove them from the school system immediately.

We need to build our communities off the grid now while we still have time.

I invite you all to join with me. You are welcome. I will share with you a vision I recently had from the Lord regarding America:

This morning in prayer and worship I had an amazing experience with the Lord. He gave me a vision and showed me fireballs (comets) (nuclear holocaust?) and asteroids hitting America. He said this is going to happen very soon and I am coming back very soon to set my kingdom down upon the earth and to destroy all of the wicked kingdoms of this world. The world is about to change forever. Everything that you have known is about to change.

He then showed me a dressing room. It was backstage and I knew that out front was the world and soon coming events. He showed me people coming into the dressing room with tattered and torn clothes on and with dirt on their faces and their hair was mangled. He told me to dress his people and to get them ready by preparing them for the things that are soon coming upon America and the world. He told me to get them dressed and prepared to meet their soon coming King. I then began to mend their garments, to wash their faces and to comb their hair.

He said "I am giving you my angel of protection". He will stay with you and protect you and my people. The Lord said I am going before you to make every crooked place straight before you. Ask of me what you need and I will do it for you.

The Lord commissioned me to gather together his people and to train and prepare them for End-Time events and to meet the Lord. This is what I am going to do. On Saturday Jan.4th, I am opening up a "Dressing Room" to help his people get prepared to meet him and prepared to endure the coming Tribulation Events.

He told me to build an "Off the Grid" community for them to run to when the Marshall Law is declared in America. He told me to build an "Underground Bunker" there and that the angel he sent to me will guard it and keep the people in it safe during the Tribulation period with food, shelter and provision.

I invite every one of you to come and be a part of preparing for the coming of the Lord. He is coming very soon. We are about to see America and the world totally change. We have entered into the Tribulation period.

Through the Spirit of the Lord I will teach you how to walk in the Spirit, to totally depend upon him to lead and guide you. I will teach you how to prepare spiritually, emotionally, and physically for the End-Times.

Jesus is calling to his people: "Come out of Babylon!"

Then I heard another voice from heaven say: "'Come out of her, my people,' so that you will not share in her sins, so that you will not receive any of her plagues. (Rev. 18:14 NIV)

How do you come out of Babylon? You pray through and get released from your lukewarm state. You prepare yourself a refuge out of the cities in the mountains with other like- minded Christians. Get away from New York. It will be burned to the ground. Get away from the coastal areas. They will be covered with water. Store up water, food, and medicines. Get your children out of the school systems. Learn to live off the grid.

My heart's desire and cry is for your understanding of End-Time events to be opened up and for you to prepare for yourself and your loved ones before it is too late for you.

It's time to prepare for the storm that is coming to America. We will watch the majority of the Christian churches and America buy into this great End-Time deception. They will back the Anti-christ spirit and workings. We are about to witness the greatest falling away of God's people from the true gospel that has ever been. Paul states that it will so great as to compare it to the horrible reign of the Anti-christ.

Let no man deceive you by any means: for that day shall not come, except there come a falling away first, and that man of sin be revealed, the son of perdition. (2 Thess. 2-3)

Jesus said the deception would be so great that even the very elect could be deceived.

Paul states prior to the coming of the lord we will witness a very great falling away of God's people from the true gospel. This happens prior to the Anti-christ being revealed. It paves the way for him.

There is only one true way to be prepared for the coming storm. You must be filled with the Holy Spirit of God and guided by him. He is the only one who knows where the places of safety will be. When God brought down the judgments upon the land of Egypt none of them fell upon the land of Goshen where God's people were living. The judgments of God that falls during the End-Times will not hurt God's people because he will lead them to places of safety. However the wrath of the Anti-christ spirit and the Anti-christ himself will bring persecution that God is not bringing upon the earth, but the Anti-christ is and God has never spared his people from tribulation and persecution. Most of the early church died from this. This sort of thing only makes the true Christians shine more brightly and live more full of love. The Bride of

Christ is polished under these conditions and she pulls closer together and makes all things common and shares her resources.

We must realize there is a difference from Gods judgments and the Anti-christ's persecution. The Anti-christ will put many Christians into concentration camps and will be-head and martyr many of them.

In order to be hidden away from both God's judgments upon the earth, in the form of meteors, comets, asteroids, global earthquakes, etc. and the Anti-christ's persecution, you will have to be hid away in God's protective "Goshen's". The only way you will know where they are is if you are being led by the Holy Spirit.

Jesus told his disciples that when they see the Anti-christ come into their temple to run for the mountains where they had a hiding place already prepared for them. God is preparing hiding places for his children all over the world. We will be protected during the End-Time events.

The sad thing is that today before all of these hard times hit so very few of God's children are being led and guided by the Holy Spirit, and many of them do not know how to be. It is the only way you will survive physically.

I have just written two books. The first one is titled "There is a River", and this book introduces you to the person of the Holy Spirit. The second book is titled "Let the River flow". It teaches you how to be led and guided by the Holy Spirit. The Lord has written these books to help his Church to get prepared for the end of days. I highly suggest that you obtain them and read them over and over again. They can be bought at Amazon.com.

There is nothing we can do on our own to be prepared for these end of day's events. There are End-Time preppers all over the world storing up commodities and guns and ammunition, but they have left Jesus out of the equation and their best efforts will only take care of them for a period of time.

This is the time to do the following:

Read my two books, and fast and pray and seek the Lord like you have never sought him before, praying for your spiritual eyes to be opened to the truth of God's word and not deception.

It's time to be led and guided by the Holy Spirit in everything you do. It's time to get your body into good health and wholeness and to lose weight, exercise, eat healthy. It's time to store up as much medicines, home remedies, and first aid as you can.

It's time to store up commodities to feed you and your loved ones for 3 ½ years. It's time to locate another group or body of Christ that you can have communion and fellowship with to pool resources and strength for the End-Times.

God is raising up Goshen's all over the world. Find one close to you now and begin to prepare with them for the coming hard times.

Do not wait. If Noah had not prepared his ark ahead of time, when the floods came his whole family would have drowned. If Joseph had not prepared ahead of time the whole land of Egypt and the surrounding nations would have starved.

The preparation must occur ahead of the event. You can't learn to dance five minutes before the prom.

The Lord has commissioned me to build End-Time Goshen's. He said he would watch over these places and keep them safe.

Just remember, that very soon, you will not be able to go to the store and buy anything without the Mark of the Beast.

You won't be able to sell anything either to make a living without it.

You need to learn to live off of the grid right now! You need to make you a place where it is self-sufficient. It needs to be a place that has a running stream, a well, solar heat, and where you can grow crops, cattle, and farm animals. You need to learn first aid, and how to survive in the wild.

These things are much easier when you join with another group in a community with the same goals and needs, but the most important thing is to make sure it is a place that the Holy Spirit has led you to, because only those places will be protected by God.

America is the Babylon spoken of in the book of Revelation. God is going to sweep across her one more time in his love and mercy pleading with her to repent, then he is going to destroy her in one hour by fire!

Judgment is coming upon America! Repent! And turn from your wicked ways! Seek the Lord while he may be found. Arouse thyself sleeping Church and rise up in the power and anointing of the Holy Spirit.

You need to find yourself a church or fellowship group that can prepare you for the coming hard times. It's time to get yourself prepared so you can protect yourself and your loved one.

In the next few years while Israel is living in safety and at rest, we the people of America are about to begin to experience great persecution from Mystery Babylon. This persecution will get so bad that many Christians will die, and be put into prisons for it.

Mystery Babylon which is the One World Church will come on the scene first. She will gain total power over the world. Those who do not join her will be persecuted and done away with. After she has gotten the world away from the true Jesus of the Bible into serving the American Jesus, then the Anti-christ will come on the scene and rule the word for three and a half years.

He will do away with Mystery Babylon who allowed all faiths to be worshipped and he will begin a new religion that only believes in him and that worships him. This is our time to prepare. It is our only time!!!

A prudent man seeth the evil, and hideth himself; But the simple pass on, and suffer for it. (Prov. 22:3)

If you live anywhere close to Denham Springs, Louisiana I invite you to come join with us as we build a city Goshen here to gather , inform, and train God's people and a mountain Goshen to run to that is off the grid with an underground safety bunker. Come and get yourself and your family informed and protected as the storm is on the horizon.

May God richly keep and bless you all.

Sincerely, a servant in Christ

Judy C. Newton

Books by Judy C. Newton

There is a River

Let the River flow

The American Jesus

Beware Of Men

End Of Days, The Anti-christ Revealed

Goshen

These books can be purchased at: www.amazon.com

Please visit our website:

www.theriverendtimechurch.com

Our Facebook page:

The River End Time Church "The Praying Preppers"

Or call us:225-243-4596

Made in the USA
San Bernardino, CA
30 December 2013